MONEY
is my
FRIEND

by Phil Laut

Nationally known financial consultant and seminar leader describes techniques that have increased the incomes of thousands of people in all walks of life.

Published by
Trinity Publications

Infinite Being
Infinite Intelligence
Infinite Manifestation

ABOUT THE AUTHOR

Phil Laut is a nationally known seminar leader and certified rebirther. He is a graduate of the Harvard Business School and served as controller in a major electronics company.

Copyright © 1978 by Phil Laut
All Right Reserved
ISBN #0-89626-030-5
Library of Congress Card Catalogue No. 79-51206

First Printing May 1979
Second Printing August 1979
Third Printing December 1979
Fourth Printing July 1980
Fifth Printing April 1981
Sixth Printing October 1981
Seventh Printing January 1982
Eighth Printing August 1982
Ninth Printing November 1982
Tenth Printing May 1983

Additional copies of *Money is My Friend* are available at bookstores throughout the United States and Canada, at most Science of Mind Churches, Churches of Religious Science and Unity Church bookstores and at locations listed in the back of the book.

TRINITY PUBLICATIONS
1636 N. CURSON AVE.
HOLLYWOOD, CALIFORNIA 90046 USA
213-876-6226

Universal Life Church
First Immortalist Congregation

TABLE OF CONTENTS

ACKNOWLEDGMENTS

I am grateful to my friend and teacher, Leonard Orr, for encouraging me to steal his ideas which are a part of this book, and I thank him for the generosity with which he shares his wisdom with me.

I want to acknowledge myself for possessing the wisdom and fortitude to publish this book. Self-publishing has already proven to be an exciting adventure.

No one writes a book alone. Many people have freely provided me with ideas and encouragement: Lucy McDowell, Leonard Orr, Bill Chappelle, Kyle Os, Sondra Ray, Bobby Birdsall, Dick Vogal, Neil Adams, Binnie Dansby, and Jim Leonard to name a few.

Also by Phil Laut:
Rebirthing—The Science of Enjoying All of Your Life by Phil Laut and Jim Leonard; also published by Trinity Publications

French Language Edition of *Money is My Friend* available from:
Les Editions M.C.L.
C. P. 402
Station H
Montreal, Que. H3G 2L1
Canada

Introduction

Welcome to the adventure of building a prosperity consciousness.

What you can expect to receive from the information presented in *Money is My Friend* is:

- A thorough understanding of the FOUR LAWS of WEALTH.
- Increased Income.
- A light-hearted attitude and sense of self-reliance about your financial problems.
- The information you need to start and prosper in the career you want.

Money is My Friend will introduce you to THE FOUR LAWS OF WEALTH. These four simple laws govern all wealth and are practiced by financially successful people, stock companies and financial institutions. The practices and techniques that are discussed in *Money is My Friend* will enable you to apply the FOUR LAWS OF WEALTH to your personal finances.

The first of the FOUR LAWS OF WEALTH is the EARNING LAW.

THE EARNING LAW is

ALL HUMAN WEALTH IS CREATED BY THE HUMAN MIND.

The application of the EARNING LAW involves the pleasurable creation of a sufficient income.

THE SPENDING LAW is

THE VALUE OF MONEY IS DETERMINED BY THE BUYER AND SELLER IN EVERY TRANSACTION.

Application of the SPENDING LAW involves enjoyment of the things that you spend money for.

THE SAVING LAW is

THE ACCUMULATION OF A SURPLUS FROM YOUR INCOME.

Application of the SAVING LAW involves saving a percentage of your income. This act results in an attitude of extra, of abundance, which you can expect to see reflected in your future income.

THE INVESTING LAW is

SPENDING YOUR CAPITAL IN YOUR NAME FOR THE PURPOSE OF INCREASING YOUR INCOME.

Application of the INVESTING LAW is a combination of the first three LAWS OF WEALTH as the factors of earning, spending and saving all come into play. Included in the explanation of the INVESTING LAW are ideas about selling and about your own business.

Money is My Friend contains an abundance of ideas, practices and techniques to make your financial life more satisfying. *Money is My Friend* has been in publication since 1979. During this time, I have discovered that the people who have benefitted the most from *Money is My Friend* have been the ones who have been willing to read it more than once. I invite you to take your time with this book. Please try out the ideas you like the best; once you have mastered a few; come back for another reading.

CHAPTER I

Prosperity Consciousness

The purpose of this book is to eliminate poverty in the world and to make abundant living socially acceptable. The least that you can do is to master the principles that are explained in here and to use them to become wealthy. For the past seven years, I have been conducting seminars and doing individual consulting with people about money. In writing this book, I have included the most valuable ideas about money that I can think of. For some readers the ideas in this book may be new or seem strange at first. Psychologists have found that as many as six repetitions of an idea are necessary before new information becomes a part of a person's consciousness. For this reason, it is a good idea to re-read this book from time to time. You will find that concepts that you missed on previous readings will flash into your consciousness as though you had never read them before. I encourage you to get your money's worth. A good way to use this book is to re-read it from time to time and make a list of the practices in here that you are not now using. Pick out the one you like the best and start using it.

This book is about achieving FINANCIAL FREEDOM. Financial Freedom is when you never do anything that you don't want to for money and you never omit doing something that you want to do because of lack of money. Another way of describing the condition of financial freedom is that money works for you, instead of you working for money. Building a PROSPERITY CONSCIOUSNESS is the way to ensure your financial success. A prosperity consciousness is the ability to function effortlessly and conveniently in the physical world, having money or not. The progressive construction of a

1

prosperity consciousness makes financial freedom a realistic possibility. You will find that a prosperity consciousness will produce cash for you every time as well as several other important benefits. I have observed that negative ideas about survival and dependency are the ones that tend to hold money problems in place. A prosperity consciousness not only makes it easy and fun to solve your money problems, but it will provide you emotional security and a pervasive sense of self-reliance.

If you plan to live in a society that uses money as a means of exchange, then it is intelligent to master money. A prosperity consciousness is having money work for you instead of you working for money. People with a prosperity consciousness know that money is one of the least important things in life. If you haven't mastered money yet, the tendency is to worry about it constantly. Constant worry does little to improve your cash flow. This book is a way out of that bind.

I have purposely made this book brief. You will find that it is packed with useful money producing ideas. For this reason I recommend you take your time in reading it and make a special note to re-read the sections that make you angry, skeptical or afraid.

CHAPTER II

The Earning Law

The progressive construction of a prosperity consciousness involves psychological and practical mastery of THE FOUR LAWS OF WEALTH. In this book you will be introduced to:

    I.   THE EARNING LAW
    II.   THE SPENDING LAW
    III.   THE SAVING LAW
    IV.   THE INVESTING LAW

The EARNING LAW is the most important. If you haven't mastered the EARNING LAW, then the others are just intellectual concepts.

In talking about the EARNING LAW I want to be very scientific. Science is concerned with determining the cause and effect of things. So we want to be very scientific here and determine the causative factor that produces wealth in every case. Once we uncover this, it will no longer be necessary for you to rely on luck or any other external factors to increase your income.

There are several popular myths that need to be dealt with on the way to uncovering THE EARNING LAW. These are the things that our parents, our teachers, our guidance counsellors and other, wise, but perhaps not so financially successful, people have taught us about money. The most popular myth that I have identified is that hard work is the causative factor that produces wealth—that earning money is an inherently

3

unpleasant activity. The statistics that I have read do not support this. The Social Security Administration tells me that the average cash assets of a person reaching age 65 in this country are $250. This is the richest country in the world, and these are people who worked for money 40 hours per week for 40 years or so. If working hard for money produced wealth, then it would produce wealth in every case. Rich people work a lot less than poor people do. The idea that hard work is required to be wealthy has been codified into the Puritan Work Ethic and its futility is daily demonstrated in the frustration of the middle-class American work-aholic. If your parent(s) came home from work tired every day, then it is likely that you borrowed this myth from them. If you are working only for the money, you have probably already discovered that money is never enough reward. Those people who work only for the money have a tendency to create debts and installment payments for the things that they have bought in an attempt to give themselves the satisfaction that they miss at work.

Another common myth about money is that it is not right to enjoy yourself and get paid for it. One day I was sitting in the Boston Garden watching a Celtics game along with fifteen thousand or so people who had paid $3.50 to $8.00 to watch the game. The spectators were all enjoying themselves. Then I noticed the ushers, all of whom looked unhappy, despite the fact that they were engaged in the same activity as the spectators—that is, sitting in a seat, watching the game. I thought it would be interesting to take a little poll. I sat down next to ten of the ushers, one at a time, and asked each of them the same question. "Are you enjoying the game?" I was a little surprised to discover that none of them even answered the question because they were too busy complaining to me about what a crummy job it was to be an usher. Ultimately, the only difference between the ushers and the spectators was that the ushers were being paid to be there and the spectators had paid to be there. I don't think that any of the ushers were millionaires. And most millionaires that I know enjoy their work much more than the ushers reported.

Another popular myth about money is that the right occupation is the key to financial success. This idea is frequently

extolled by guidance counsellors and matchbook covers—
"Twelve Ways to Success—be a surveyor, a motel operator,
etc." An extreme example is in the movie "The Graduate,"
where Dustin Hoffman hears "plastics" whispered in his ear. If
you think about it for a few moments, you can probably identify
people who are financially successful and people who are not, in
almost every occupation you can think of. Additionally, there
are people who are financially successful in some of the most
improbable occupations that you can imagine. If you would like
to be convinced of this, then you can sit down and read the
Yellow Pages of the telephone directory someday.

Another common myth about money is that education will
ensure your financial success. This idea is especially common
among educators. If this were true ultimately, then college
professors would be the richest people in the country. Most
educators I know are poor with the exception of a few who
have written successful books. One day I accompanied a
friend when she was visiting the employment security office
in San Francisco to pick up her unemployment check. Since I
had never visited an unemployment office before, I thought it
would be an interesting adventure. The lines were long and
after a while I got tired of standing around, so I decided to
take another poll. I went up and down the lines of people
waiting for their unemployment checks and asked the same
question of about fifty individuals: "What did you do for
money before you were unemployed?" Almost all the
answers were different. I found unemployed waiters,
waitresses, accountants, factory workers, secretaries, there
was even a guy there who was a marine designer with a PhD.
in marine engineering.

Another common myth about money is that there is not
enough to go around—that the more you have, the less there is
for everyone else, so that it is better to be poor and righteous
than rich and evil. People with this idea usually resent rich
people. Ironically, it is this resentment of rich people that keeps
them poor, because they would resent themselves a lot more if
they became rich. The truth is that money was invented by
people for their own convenience, and since your money comes
from people, the only thing you can do with it is give it to other

people. This is true unless you are in the habit of stuffing your mattress with your extra greenbacks. If you spend money, you prosper other people; if you save money, you prosper others because the bank takes the money you deposit and loans it to others; and if you invest money, then you are simply giving it to someone else to spend in your name. I like what Alan Watts said about money. He asked his father how come there was a Depression. His father told him it was because they had run out of money. This seemed ridiculous to him; like a carpenter showing up for work one day and being told that he couldn't work that day because they had run out of inches.

Money is blamed for personal and social problems that are caused by lack of money or love of money. One of the factors that prompted me to write this book was the realization that money cannot cure poverty. It is only necessary to study the Federal anti-poverty programs of the mid 1960's to discover this for yourself. The basic idea of the anti-poverty program was that the problem with poor people was that they had no money. This leads to the erroneous conclusion that the way to solve the problem is to give poor people money. The program didn't work as intended—if it had there would be no poor people now.

There is already enough money to solve poverty several times over, and it is only practical education and banishment of erroneous thinking about money that will cure poverty.

THE EARNING LAW STATED IS THAT ALL HUMAN WEALTH IS CREATED BY THE HUMAN MIND.

This means that thought is the causative factor that creates wealth in every case. Money is composed of paper, metal and numbers—all of which are totally effect and without creative power. The key to wealth is learning how to take charge of your mind, learning how to process your mind with affirmations, studying and releasing yourself from the major inhibitors of the mind and learning to better use your imagination. Said most simply, increasing your wealth is a matter of increasing the quality of your thoughts—increasing the quality of your thoughts about money, increasing the quality of your thoughts about yourself and increasing the quality of your thoughts about what you do for money.

The study of thought is philosophy and the study of how thoughts affect our behavior is psychology. The next two chapters establish a base in these two subjects that will be used throughout the rest of the book.

CHAPTER III

A Short Course in Philosophy

The purpose of philosophy is to study and describe thought and to create generally applicable ideas that will enable us to increase the quality of our lives. Philosophy with any other purpose is tyranical dogmatism. The obvious place to begin a philosophical discussion is with the physical universe, simply because it is so obvious. By the physical universe, I mean your body, your car, your dog, the tree outside and most important for the purposes of this book, your bank account.

One of the properties of the physical universe is that it does not have the power to create itself. Rocks do not create rocks, your body does not create your body. You can see this by examining a corpse. A corpse weighs the same and contains the same chemical elements as a live body—so there must be something mystical or at least invisible going on that is related to life.

Another property of the physical universe is that it is orderly. The planets proceed around the sun in the same orderly manner as electrons proceed around the nucleus of atoms. Your life is ordered by your thoughts. My friend Bobby Birdsall describes this very simply by saying that the mind is composed of two parts—the Thinker and the Prover. The Thinker thinks and the Prover proves whatever the Thinker thinks. The Prover does not care what you think; you can think whatever you want to and the Prover will prove it to be true. The job of the Prover is to keep you from going insane; because if you went around all day thinking 'People will hurt me' and you discovered that everywhere you went people loved you, this would drive you nuts.

The physical universe is created out of your thoughts. Since you can think anything that you want to in infinite variety and in infinite combination, it seems that your thoughts must come from somewhere that is infinite. The infinite has the property of Oneness. This means that there can only be one infinite, or it could not be infinite.

You can think of a Three Part Creative Process that starts with the infinite which is the source of your thoughts. The second element is thought and the third element is the physical universe, the result of the thought. The following diagram depicts the Creative Process and lists some of the different names that people have used for each of the three elements.

THE CREATIVE PROCESS

Flows from left to right on this diagram. The words and phrases in each column are each different ways of describing an element of the Creative Process.

The Infinite	Thought	The Physical Universe
The Source	Knowledge	The Comforter
The Force	Idea	The Holy Spirit
The Great Spirit	Concept	Your Bank Account
God	Education	Your Body
The Father	Religion	Your Car
Infinite Being	Son	Your Lover
Infinite Potential	Attitude	Your House
The Thinker	Doing	Your Personal Reality
Spirit	Infinite	Having
Being	Intelligence	Infinite Manifestation

One of the characteristics of the Creative Process is that it always works. It worked last year, it works now, it will continue to work next year, it works in New York City, it works in the middle of the ocean and it works in outer space. As a student I was always interested in learning the laws of the universe. Whenever the professor would describe a scientific law, I would ask whether it worked all the time. The professor never said yes, because it seems that there are exceptions to all scientific laws.

Conscious use of the Creative Process puts at your command the power of a philosophical law that always works.

10

There are no problems that you cannot solve with the Creative Process; it puts you in charge of your life and will make you realize that since you are the Creator of your life, you can create the way you would like it. The next three principles are practical applications of the Creative Process. Once you master them, you can have anything you want in life.

THE SELF-ANALYSIS PRINCIPLE

Applying the self-analysis principle is asking yourself, what have I been thinking that has created my life the way that it is? This principle is the basis of classical psycho-analysis. Most people do not do this because they are afraid to find out what they have been thinking. Negative thoughts only create negative results as long as you think them, so it won't hurt you to find out what they are, especially after you master the next principle which enables you to change your thoughts.

THE SUGGESTION PRINCIPLE

The suggestion principle is asking yourself 'what would I like to think in order to create my life the way I would like it.' You can apply the suggestion in several ways; by reading, by listening, by watching, by writing and by talking. The suggestion principle enables you to increase the quality of your thoughts by reading high quality books (like this one), by listening to cassette tapes and self-improvement seminars and by writing affirmations. An affirmation is a high quality thought that you like well enough to immerse in your consciousness. Affirmations regarding the EARNING LAW.

1) I deserve to be prosperous and wealthy.
(If money makes you feel guilty because you don't feel like you deserve it, then it is difficult to increase your income, because if you did you would just feel more guilty.)
2) It is OK for me to be paid for enjoying myself.
(Struggling and engaging in unpleasant activities just for the money makes it difficult to become wealthy.)
3) My personal connection to infinite being and infinite intelligence is adequate enough to yield me a huge personal fortune.
(Your imagination is the source of your income and the in-

11

finite being and infinite intelligence is the source of the ideas that fill your imagination.)

Writing is the fastest way to incorporate these ideas into your consciousness. I suggest that you put your name in these affirmations to make them more personal and write them in all three persons. (For simplicity, affirmations in this book are in the first person. You can convert them into the other two persons yourself.) For example,

I Phil deserve to be prosperous and wealthy. (First person)
Phil, you deserve to be prosperous and wealthy. (Second person)
Phil deserves to be prosperous and wealthy. (Third person)

Leave a space at the right hand side of your paper for the response that your mind gives you to the new thought in the affirmation and write down the responses that have emotional impact. One of the characteristics of the mind is that it tends to be associative, so it is impossible to be writing "I deserve to be prosperous and wealthy" without negative ideas that you may have about money coming to your attention.

Sample affirmation exercise:

Affirmation	Response
I deserve to be prosperous and wealthy.	On yeah?
I deserve to be prosperous and wealthy.	Why am I doing this?
I deserve to be prosperous and wealthy.	I feel tired
I deserve to be prosperous and wealthy.	?
I deserve to be prosperous and wealthy.	I don't want to work that hard.
Phil, you deserve to be prosperous and wealthy.	Who says?
Phil, you deserve to be prosperous and wealthy.	Not yet.
Phil, you deserve to be prosperous and wealthy.	Maybe I'll try it.
Phil, you deserve to be prosperous and wealthy.	My father told me I had to work hard.
Phil, you deserve to be prosperous and wealthy.	Why not?

Phil deserves to be prosperous and wealthy.	What will my friends think?
Phil deserves to be prosperous and wealthy.	No one ever told me so before.
Phil deserves to be prosperous and wealthy	I'm starting to believe it.

The purpose of using all three persons in affirmations is to make it easy to discover and let go of your negative ideas no matter where they came from—whether you thought them up yourself, whether someone else told them to you or whether someone else said them about you. It is a very good idea to breathe fully and deeply while you are writing affirmations. If you get the same response over and over, it is a good idea to invent an affirmation that is the opposite of that response. For example, if 'I don't want to work that hard' is a continuing response, then take 'I deserve to be paid for enjoying myself' as your affirmation.

THE GOALS PRINCIPLE

The goals principle is asking yourself 'what would I like to create to have what I like'. The purpose of the goals principle is to give your mind an opportunity to create for yourself. (Some people would much rather complain about what they have than ask for what they want.) Having only realistic goals is not recommended. Realistic goals are based on your view of what can happen based on what has happened in the past. Now that you are increasing the quality of your thoughts, there is no limit as to what can happen. I suggest that you make a list of goals— all the things that you would like to be do and have. Another way to do it is to think of the different areas of your life and write down what you would like. It is a good idea to have commercial goals for your business, social goals for your relationships, psychosomatic goals for your body and intellectual goals for skills that you would like to acquire.

MONEY AND SPIRITUALITY

There have been some negative ideas floating around for a

very long time that affect spiritual people as they work at building their prosperity consciousness and creating abundance in their lives. Some of these negative ideas are that money and spirituality don't mix, that the material world is an illusion, that "money is the root of all evil." These ideas are based on the old view that God and Man are separate and that it's holier to wait to experience abundance until you're *there* (with God in Heaven) rather than enjoy it here and now on earth. Although Western religions paid lip service to the idea that God is everywhere, the fact that God might be riding around with you in your Mercedes, and enjoying it too, was not well publicized.

The truth is that the universe is made up of Divine Substance —which is God and nothing but God. You can't get away from God by being materialistic; you are immersed in God and there's no way out. Furthermore, there is not one single particle of the physical world that is not in essence OK with God.

Having a prosperity consciousness enables you to function easily and effortlessly in the material world. The material world is God's world, and you are God being you. If you are experiencing pleasure and freedom and abundance in your life, then you are expressing your true spiritual nature. And the more spiritual you are, the more you deserve prosperity.

When the charge is gone from your experience of money, it becomes highly abstract and mystical stuff. It symbolizes both the infinite and the finite. It is the power of God on the material plane, which is the power of wealth. It allows you to materialize and dematerialize things at will, just like God. It allows you to create beauty in your life and in the lives of others. Your use of the power of wealth can be an act of faith, love and thanksgiving in every instance.

Affirm your connection to Infinite Being and Infinite Intelligence often. Your consciousness of your connection to Infinite Being and Infinite Intelligence is your most valuable personal asset.

Money Affirmations

1) I deserve to be prosperous and wealthy.
2) I deserve to be paid for enjoying myself.

3) My personal connection to infinite being and infinite intelligence is adequate enough to yield me a large personal fortune.

4) Money is my friend.

5) I have plenty of money.

6) I am at one with the power that is materializing my desires.

7) My presence alone produces valuable results.

8) My financial life is easy.

9) It is OK for me to exceed my goals.

10) Beauty, power and harmony abound in my mind.

11) It is fun for me to be a wealthy (wo)man.

12) I now allow others to support my financial success.

13) My well-being has nothing to do with my financial success.

14) I forgive myself for using money to control people.

15) I forgive myself for wasting money.

CHAPTER IV

Psychology and Prosperity

Psychology is the study of how thoughts affect people's behavior. In this chapter you will learn about the effect of thought structures on prosperity and learn about the major inhibitors of the human mind—THE FIVE BIGGIES.

The thoughts that cause people the most trouble are the ones that are connected with survival or with security. The tendency is to cling to even negative thoughts that you think are necessary for your survival. When you sleep, you lapse into a pre-verbal state of consciousness where for the most part you do not have conscious control of your thoughts. This fact should indicate that the world is safe for you, that there are no thoughts necessary to your survival. The repetitive impact of affirmations on your consciousness enable you to uncover and free yourself from negative repetitive thoughts.

Another category of thoughts that cause problems are the thoughts related to getting approval or love from other people. These are related to survival thoughts because in our infantile helplessness (when thought patterns were first formed), it appeared that our survival was dependent upon the approval (or at least the sufferance) of others. Some examples of thoughts like this are:

> I have to fight for what I want.
> No one wants me.
> I am helpless and dependent.
> It is not safe to be truthful.
> etc, etc.

17

The key here is to realize that you are your own source of love. It is impossible to love someone else more than you love yourself; it is impossible to experience more love from someone else than you are willing to give yourself. Another way of saying this is that once you begin to enjoy your own company, it becomes a lot easier to enjoy the company of someone else.

THE FIVE BIGGIES.

In my consulting work I have found that the major inhibitors of the human mind could be classified into the Five Biggies. The Five Biggies are Birth Experience, Parental Disapproval Syndrome, Specific Negatives, Unconscious Death Urge and Other Lifetimes.

BIRTH EXPERIENCE

Birth was a confusing event that marked the end of a nine month period of relaxation in the womb. In the womb, the kundalini energy which built your body in the first place flowed uninhibitedly, all of your needs were met without your doing anything, and life had a sense of timelessness and oneness about it. Birth was your first social experience, that is the first experience you had with people that you could see. The conclusions that you made about life at birth are important to know about and to change in developing a prosperity consciousness. Almost everyone learned how to breathe after the umbilical cord was cut. This means that breathing was learned in fear and panic of death. For this reason almost everyone breathes less than fully and freely. Breath is the connection between the visible and the invisible. Breath is the connection between the God within and the God without. Breathing is the activity that we do the most of. Mastering your breath is an eminently practical thing to do whether you would like to increase your income or not. Solitude is joyous if you are breathing fully and freely. If you are not then solitude becomes loneliness and distressing because of the fact that the struggle that is required for you to breathe comes to your attention. Rebirthing is the technique that is receiving world-wide acceptance as a method of freeing the breath from the negative experience of birth. Rebirthing involves relaxing and breathing in the presense of a Rebirther who acts as a breathing coach. Currently there are over 2,000 Rebirthers offering this technique to people. For more information about Rebirthing, I suggest that you read *Rebirthing—The Science of Enjoying All of Your Life* by Phil Laut and Jim Leonard, published by Trinity Publications, or write to one of the addresses in the back of the book.

I want to suggest a simple exercise so that you can get an idea of the power of your breath. Lie down in a relaxed position and close your eyes. Take twenty even medium-speed breaths in and out through your mouth being careful to connect the inhale with the exhale and the exhale with the inhale in a continuous rhythm. Then take four long, easy breaths. Then back to the twenty medium speed breaths as before and so forth. A few minutes of this exercise will give you a hint of the pleasure you can experience in a Rebirthing session. After you have been Rebirthed, it is possible to do this for hours at a time. The pleasure is probably more than you can imagine.

The essence of the birth experience is unexplained emotions. Said another way, it is the confusion between love and pain. This confusion manifests in people's lives with the idea that it is possible to suffer enough to earn bliss. If you think you can struggle enough to earn bliss, you are a bit like the ancient pagans who thought they could prevent earthquakes by sacrificing goats. The trouble with this way of thinking is that you can never relax, because no one ever comes along to tell you that you have sacrificed enough goats.

As you begin to unravel significant events in your personal history—the events surrounding birth and parental conditioning, you will discover that the events are not the important things. The events, no matter how terrifying, are over and done; they are in the past. Uncovering the ideas and rules about life that we made as a result of these events is the important thing. The tendency is to keep operating on these unconscious rules until they are consciously changed.

When I started to travel around the country conducting my seminars, I was successful right from the beginning no matter where I went. However, I found that the seminars that I conducted when I was at home were poorly attended. It was interesting for me to see that a teacher of prosperity principles would have his income go almost to zero whenever he went home. When I started thinking about this problem I remembered that when I was a child, my father had commuted from New Jersey to New York City to work. I thought that I was copying his example of having to travel away from home to earn an income. I started writing affirmations like, "I am not my father. It is easy for me to produce an income at home." Nothing happened. The next time I went home, my income was even less than it had been before. By this time I had had enough Rebirthing sessions that it was pretty easy for me to recall incidents from my birth and infancy. When I started to think about this problem again, I recalled lying in the nursery just after my birth. The door to the room opened and a hospital attendant walked in. I jumped in fright at the prospect of being mishandled again, until I took a second look and noticed that the attendant was about forty feet away. My next thought was, 'I don't have to worry about him, I only have to worry about the people close to me.' I knew this was related to my problem with my income, so I took the affirmation, "I am willing to trust people near me." The next time I went home, my business there started providing me with the abundance that I had previously enjoyed only on the road.

This story contains an important lesson about the use of affirmations. Affirmations always work. If your affirmations are not producing the results that you want (as mine did not in this story) then it is clear to you that you are not using the right affirmations.

THE PARENTAL DISAPPROVAL SYNDROME

The essence of the parental disapproval syndrome is the idea that love is something that you can only get if you earn it. Another way of saying this is that the parental disapproval syndrome is the belief in limits that can be overcome by struggle. Regarding money, it is the idea that it is necessary to perform some unpleasant task to earn money and if you are lucky, you might get to enjoy spending it. The parental disapproval syndrome is the biggest biggy regarding money.

For this reason I have devoted the next chapter to exercises so that you can unravel it in your consciousness. Also the chapter after next is devoted to several cases of the parental disapproval syndrome. Children are unabashed expressions of divinity and are very loving. The close connection that children feel with their parents, especially with their mother causes them to imitate their parents. Because of their uninhibited intuitive abilities, children tend not only to imitate their parents' behavior, but also their thoughts. To most parents it is a little disconcerting to see their subconscious acted out in three dimensions. Parents react to their discomfort by providing their children with a bunch of rules about how to act—rules for right thinking, rules for the right use of time, rules about reward and punishment, all of which impose limits and act to inhibit the divinity of the child. After a while, most children give up trying overtly to get what they want outside of the rules that have been established, once they realize that it is not safe to be a rebel, at least openly. Since it was not safe to express hostility that you felt as a child, it is probably suppressed in your consciousness, from where it operates without your awareness, and apparently without your control. It is the hostility that people feel toward their spouses, their children, their bosses, the government and so forth. The value of understanding the parental disapproval syndrome in your consciousness is that it is much easier to dissolve the hostility and let it go once you understand the source of it. It is a good idea to close your eyes and imagine your parents as small children. This will give you the opportunity to tell them what you always wanted to in a safe way. I am only being a little facetious when I say that in order to be a millionaire, all you have to do is learn how to love your parents. This means loving them because you want to, not beause they told you that is what you ought to do.

SPECIFIC NEGATIVES

Specific negatives are the favorite negative ideas that people use to beat themselves up with. Whenever you feel depressed, write down all of your thoughts. This will transfer your depression from subjective reality to objective reality and make it easy for you to see the cause of your depression. After writing down your thoughts for fifteen minutes or so, you will probably say to yourself, 'No wonder I am depressed, anyone with thoughts like that would feel depressed'. The next step is to take the negative thoughts you were just thinking as indicated on the paper and invert them into affirmations and then write the affirmations. I have found that this simple little exercise cures depression every time.

UNCONSCIOUS DEATH URGE

Just as a person's ideas about money are the cause of his experience of money, so are a person's ideas about death the cause of his experience about death. Many of us have been trained to believe in the inevitability of death. This training frequently results in an entire belief system about death. With the idea of life extension, rejuvenation and physical immortality becoming more popular, this belief system can be challenged. The unconscious death urge is the name I call the belief system about death. It is a belief system based on scarcity, lack and limitation. Freeing yourself from its influence will increase your prosperity to no end.

The essence of the unconscious death urge is the helplessness and hopelessness surrounding the idea that you can't even earn the love that you want. When I first heard about physical immortality, I thought it was a pretty far out idea, something I could think about after I had mastered money, after I had the perfect relationship and the house of my dreams. I found that after one exposure to the idea that I thought about it a lot. One thing I am sure about is that I am a very practical person. So I started thinking about the practical aspects of physical immortality. I realized that the belief in the inevitability of death was a statement that the universe is a hostile place—that there is something waiting to kill you without your permission. If you have this idea, then the intelligent thing to do is to protect yourself from death. The constant effort required to protect yourself causes tension in your body.If you think that death is inevitable, then don't be surprised if people are hostile to you. Religion has never adequately explained the inevitability of death. Maybe it is just the belief in the inevitability of death that causes death to occur. In any case, you have nothing to lose by affirming your right and ability to live forever. The peace and certainty of life that will begin to inhabit your consciousness will make it easier to increase your income or anything else you want to do.

I have worked with clients whose death urges were active during the time we worked together. Just the idea of physical immortality enabled them to double their incomes, because it freed their minds from the worrying that they had been doing about death. Mastering physical immortality seems to be a three-part process.

1) Master immortalist philosophy. (There are a couple of books mentioned in the bibliography to get you started.)
2) Free yourself from your own personal death urge, by rooting out any loyalty to death that still inhabits your consciousness.
3) Practical mastery of your body.

OTHER LIFETIMES

Other lifetimes are highly overrated as causative factors in this lifetime. Among the thousands of people that I have worked with, I only encountered one person for whom another lifetime as the major psychological causative factor in this lifetime. For this reason, I am willing to consider their importance. The parental disapproval syndrome is the biggest biggy, however, and I have noticed that the people who are very intent on blaming karma for their problems are the same ones who think it is imperative to love their parents. This makes them much more willing to blame karma than their parents.

Freeing your mind from the effect of THE FIVE BIGGIES will increase your wealth, love, happiness and health.

THE TRUTH ABOUT EMOTIONS

The truth about emotions is that bliss is your natural emotional state. Negative emotions only possess the power that you give them. You give them this power by clinging to them. The tendency to cling to them is based on the belief that they are necessary for your survival or necessary for you to get love, as described at the beginning of this chapter.

23

Emotions are bodily reaction to thoughts we are afraid to know about. Emotions appear to be the context within which thoughts are held; this is an apparency, however, caused by the momentary power of the emotion, which blocks your mind from seeing the thought that caused the emotion in the first place. When you are willing to relax into your emotions, that is sink in to them instead of running way, it becomes easy to see the thoughts that cause them.

Your natural state as a powerful, intelligent being is bliss. Bliss is a pervasive feeling of well-being for no apparent reason. Other descriptions of this feeling are peace, joy, acceptance, calm, relaxation, samadhi, love, power—all of which result in feeling loving. Negative emotions occasion feeling unloving. The prevalent thought accompanying a negative emotion is the thought of being helpless to change it. In fact, it is the thought of helplessness that will act to keep the negative emotion in place. The following table is designed to give you a clear understanding of negative emotions and make it easy to free yourself from them.

← **FOLD OUT**

Remedy	Sample Affirmations
Forgiveness	I forgive my parents and doctor for the pain they caused me at birth. I acknowledge their love for me and mine for them.
	I forgive myself for not receiving what I wanted.
Safety	As long as I breathe, my body is safe. Fear is safe for me.
	The margin of safety increases in my environment every day.
Free the other person or thing from your need.	I am a self-determined person and I allow others the same right.
Self-reliance	The more freedom I allow others, the more freedom there is for me. The less I need others, the easier it is for them to love me.
Self-forgiveness	I am innocent. I am a child of God. All my desires are holy and they always have been.
Let go of your desire to prove something.	It is easy for people to see how wonderful I am. I new feel comfortable in the presence of everyone.
Self-love	I like myself. I am a lovable person.
	I no longer have to earn money or love. I am lovable and capable.
Remind yourself that you deserve it.	I deserve to be prosperous and wealthy. I deserve love whether I am successful or not.

Negative Emotion	Definition
Anger	Intention contaminated with the idea of helplessness.
Rage	Extreme anger.
Resentment	Long standing anger.
Fear	Anger with the idea that they will hit you back harder. When you feel fear, the anger is suppressed and you are only in touch with the desire to protect yourself.
Sadness	Rage at being attached.
Grief	Extreme sadness. Rage with regard to loss.
Jealousy	Present time fear of future time loss. This usually involves seeing someone else have the fun that you are not willing to allow yourself.
Guilt	Fear of punishment, usually resulting in self-punishment before someone else can do it.
Pride	Temporary feeling of well-being, at the expense of another.
Apathy	Rage turned against yourself in the form of self-hate.
Admiration	The highest form of apathy. Admiration is inactive. You can admire someone forever and it will never do you a bit of of good.
Lust	Exaggerated alienation—a form of resentment bringing past losses into the present.
Greed	Lust with regard to money.
Gluttony	Lust with regard to food.
Smoking	Lust with regard to breathing.

More Affirmations

BIRTH
1. I forgive my parents and doctor for the pain they caused me at birth. I acknowledge their love for me and mine for them.
2. I survived my birth. I have the right to be here.
3. I am glad I was born and so is everyone else.
4. I am now breathing fully and freely.
5. I no longer fear irreparable damage.
6. I now feel loved and connected with my parents, my friends and everyone who is important to me.

RELATIONSHIPS
1. I am no longer afraid of my parents' disapproval.
2. I am no longer afraid of my father's disapproval.
3. I am no longer afraid of my mother's disapproval.
4. Disapproval is OK with me.
5. I receive assistance and co-operation from those people everywhere necessary to achieve my desired result.
6. Everything works out more exquisitely than I plan it.
7. I am willing to allow more bliss, love and money into my life than I could imagine before.
8. I am now willing to succeed.

ALIVENESS
1. My infinite life stream has the ability to heal every cell in my body.
2. Since I am the person who knows the most about my body, it is easy for me to heal it.
3. I can live forever on bacon and eggs and chocolate cream pie.
4. My wealth contributes to my aliveness and to the aliveness of others.
5. I am at cause over money.
6. I am at cause over my body.

Affirmations from Leonard Orr

CREATIVE SELF-IMAGE
1. I, (your name) , like myself. I am a lovable person.
2. I am now highly pleasing to myself.
3. I am highly pleasing to myself in the presence of others.
4. I am highly pleasing to others and others are highly pleasing to me.
5. I am a self-determined person and I allow others the same right.
6. I have the right to say NO to people without losing their love.
7. Other people have the right to say NO to me without hurting me.
8. I like myself, therefore I like others.
9. I like myself, therefore others like me.
10. I like others, therefore others like me.
11. I like others, therefore others like themselves.
12. The more I like myself, the more others like themselves.

FOR SUPPRESSED HOSTILITY
1. I forgive my parents and others for their ignorant behavior toward me.
2. I forgive myself for my ignorant reactions toward them.
3. I forgive myself for hating my parents and other people.
4. I forgive others for hating me.
5. I forgive myself for not hating my parents and other people when it was appropriate, or when they deserved it.
6. I'm glad other people don't always express their hostility towards me when I think I deserve it.
7. I now feel loved and appreciated by my parents, my friends and everyone who is important to me.
8. I have the right and the ability to express my hostility without losing people's love, and I take responsibility to clean up the mess and restore harmony when appropriate.
9. I no longer have to be a nice guy to succeed with people.
10. I now forgive the ignorance of my doctor and parents for the pain they caused me at birth.

11. I'm glad to be out of the womb so that I can express myself fully and freely.

More Affirmations from Leonard Orr

GENERAL ALIVENESS ENRICHMENT
1. My mind is centered in infinite intelligence that knows my good; I am one with the creative power that is materializing all my desires.
2. All the cells of my body are daily bathed in the perfection of my divine being.
3. I have enough time, energy, wisdom and money to accomplish all my desires.
4. I am always in the right place at the right time, successfully engaged in the right activity.
5. I am alive now; therefore my life urges are stronger than my death urges. As long as I continue to strengthen my life urges and weaken my death urges, I will continue to live in increasing health and youthfulness.
6. Life itself is eternal, and I am life. My mind as the thinking quality of life is also eternal; therefore, my living flesh has a natural built-in tendency to live forever in perfect health and youthfulness.
7. My physical body is a safe and pleasurable place for me to be. The entire universe exists for the purpose of supporting my physical body and providing a pleasurable place for me to express myself through it.
8. I now receive assistance and co-operation from people.
9. My days and nights are filled with physical and mental pleasures.
10. I now give and receive love freely.
11. The more I win, the better I feel about letting others win. The better I feel about letting others win, the more I win; therefore, I win all the time.
12. I daily make valuable contributions to the alivenesss of myself, to others and to humanity.
13. I no longer have to ask permission to do the things that I know should be done.

CHAPTER V

Increasing Your Income

Increasing your income is a matter of using your imagination in a practical and pleasurable way. Almost none of the training we received at school was in the use of creative imagination, because schools taught us to be analytical; which is to observe something that someone else created and describe its causes and effects in detail. In this chapter there are several exercises that you can do to stimulate your imagination. Many people are unaccustomed to thinking creatively, so I have designed the exercises in a way that they will become easier with a little practice. It is a good idea to pick an exercise that you like and do it once per day for a week in order to get the maximum value from it.

THE PERFECT CAREER FOR YOU

1.   Take two minutes and write down your ten favorite pleasures.
2.   Review the list and select the very favorite pleasure that you are willing to receive money for.
3.   Take two minutes and make a list of ten ways that you can provide a service for people by performing your favorite pleasure that you are willing to receive money for.
4.   Review the second list and pick out your favorite way of providing a service for people. What you have before you is your favorite money making idea.
5.   Take another two minutes to make a list of ten things that you are willing to do to make your favorite money making idea into a financial success.

6. THE ACID TEST Now that you have an idea of what you can do to make your favorite money making idea a financial success, ask yourself whether you are willing to stick with it, no matter what it takes, until you receive your first $100 from it. If you are not willing to do this, then you certainly don't yet have an idea that you like well enough to succeed with. If your answer to the acid test is no, go back to step 1 and start the exercise again.

Frequently people switch jobs or careers because they feel like they have failed. If you make a habit of only devoting yourself to ideas that you like so well that you are willing to stick with them until you receive your first $100, you will never feel like you failed again. After receiving your first $100, you can decide whether you want to continue with the idea—but you will be making the choice from the position of having succeeded.

7. If the answer to the acid test is yes, simply take the list that you made in step 5 and make it into a personal calendar or schedule for yourself and start doing the things on the list.

CREATIVE SOLUTIONS TO FINANCIAL PROBLEMS

When you are faced with a financial problem, the common tendency is to get out your checkbook and your calculator and feverishly begin to add numbers. It is impossible to solve financial problems with money. Your imagination has the solution to all of your financial problems and if you want it to give you creative solutions, then you must ask it creative questions. The exercise that will bring solutions to your financial problems every time is:

Sit down and make a list headed, "Ten ways I can produce an extra $ _____ before _____." The amount of money and the date that you use are up to you, as you become more familiar with the exercise, it will be easy to increase the amount of money and to shorten the time. It is common for people to start with, "Ten ways I can produce an extra $15 by the end of next week."

HOW TO MAXIMIZE YOUR INCOME WORKING FOR A COMPANY OR OTHER INSTITUTION

The way to maximize your income working for someone else is to assume that you own the place and from that position do whatever it is that needs to be done. In order to do this, you must realize that job descriptions whether formally written down or not are *not* exclusive. What I mean by this is that I never read a job description that included the phrase "and that is all." Make a list entitled "Ten things I would like to do to have this place run more smoothly." It is OK to tell people what you are doing, but it is by no means necessary. Do not worry about being compensated for the extra service that you are providing; because you are building personal certainty about your ability to make a contribution. Once you have this certainty, you can turn it into cash any time you want to, whether you are compensated for it in your present job or not. Remember, the company that you work for is your company. If you work for IBM, then IBM is your company—for sure it is the only company that you have.

SELF-EMPLOYMENT

The reason that so few people are self-employed is that their parents told them never to do anything without instructions or permission. Employees frequently set up their employers as parent substitutes and experience the same dependency relationship with their employers that they had with their parents; and feel the resentment toward their employer that results in all dependency relationships. Sometimes I am amazed that business works as well as it does.

Ultimately the only difference between self-employment and working for someone else is that the self-employed person sells his services to many customers. The principles in the previous section are designed to enable you to adopt a self-employment mentality whether you are self-employed or not.

Most self-employed people work harder and longer than company-employed people. In fact, if most self-employed people went down to the local phone company to apply for a job and were told that they would have to work as hard as they do for themselves, they would quickly leave in search for a more benevolant employer. The greatest joy of self-employment is the ability to establish your own work schedule. If you are self-employed, you will find that an hour per week sitting under a tree or taking a walk will do more for your income than working an extra two hours. This is because creative ideas spring to your

35

awareness most easily when your mind and body are relaxed. While I was in the computer business, I got my best ideas while taking walks.

UNEMPLOYMENT

The purpose of unemployment and welfare benefits is to provide people a cash flow while they take the time to increase their self-esteem enough to pleasurably create a new cash flow. Regrettably, most welfare recipients and most welfare employees are not aware of this purpose. The participants in the welfare game usually resent each other and most recipients are so angry about being on welfare that they spend the checks as fast as they receive them, which tends to keep them on welfare. I have received letters from welfare mothers with five children and an estranged husband who have successfully used the principles described in this book to create their own business and get off welfare. Welfare is a wonderful invention. Since welfare was invented we have not had a single severe economic depression. Welfare was probably invented by the rich. During the 1930's the rich people realized that when the poor people had no income, it was impossible for them to purchase the goods produced by the rich; so the rich people didn't have an income either. The welfare system makes it possible for the economy to keep going regardless of the economic conditions. The sooner everyone realizes this, the sooner welfare will be unnesessary.

STARTING OVER

What keeps a lot of people poor is their fear of starting over. Rarely do I meet someone who has continuously engaged in the same occupation since birth; therefore everyone has already demonstrated the ability to start over. Mastering something and moving on to something else is a natural tendency of successful persons. If you master the PERFECT CAREER FOR YOU exercise at the beginning of this chapter, you can create a new job for yourself every day if you want to, and be financially successful, too.

Do not wait until you are *ready* to start a new career. This is like standing at the edge of the high diving board waiting for it to feel right before you jump off. Let's face it, jumping off high diving boards is scary, even after you have done it a few times.

LAZINESS LEADS TO SELF-ESTEEM LEADS TO RICHES

Mastering laziness with self-esteem is an important factor in increasing your income. You can practice this by staying in bed for a whole day on regular intervals until you can do it without feeling guilty. It has always been interesting to me to observe that the only time that most people will allow themselves the simple pleasure of relaxing in bed all day is when they are sick. When people are willing to give themselves this pleasure when they are well, they frequently find that they are sick a lot less often. I found that it took me several attempts to master this practice, because at around 4 P.M., as I was lying there, my mind would become filled with all the things I should be doing and I would find myself downstairs doing them. The first time I stayed in bed for a whole day I was surprised to wake up the next morning and see that the world still worked; the garbage had been collected, people were going to work and children were going to school—all of this still happened without my attention. This took a big load off my shoulders.

Since the essence of the Parental Disapproval Syndrome is the idea that love is something you must earn, loving yourself while you are doing nothing is the ultimate practice of self-esteem.

SELF-ESTEEM

Self-esteem is the result of the relationship that you have with yourself. Another way of saying this is that self-esteem is the thoughts and attitudes that you have about yourself. Commonly, self-esteem was randomly formed during childhood and has received little attention since. You are the person that you spend the most time with. It is impossible to love someone else more than you love yourself and it is impossible to accept more love from someone else than you are willing to receive from yourself. One time a woman stood up in one of my seminars and it was very clear that she had received the full implication of my comments about self-esteem when she said, "You know, the only problem with going on vacation is that I have to take myself along." Whether it is your desire to increase your income, to have better relationships, to master your body or whatever, the value of increasing your self-esteem cannot be over-estimated. Money will not add to your self-esteem, it works the other way around.

EXERCISES TO INCREASE YOUR SELF-ESTEEM

1.   Buy a personal calendar book and put in it only the things you really want to do.

2.   Whenever you have a thought that starts with
     'I have to. . .'
     'I ought to. . .'
     'I need to. . .'
     'I should. . .'
     'I'd better. . .'
change it to:
     'I want to. . .'
and then ask yourself whether the thought you just had is true.

3.   Give yourself the simple pleasures of life in abundance.
     Take a bath daily.
     Stay in bed all day once per week.
     Get a massage weekly.

4.   Go first class. Make your meal selections in restaurants by looking only at the left side of the menu. Going first class may take a little practice if lack of money has always been the basis of your financial decisions.

5.   Always speak the best of yourself and others and expect others to do the same.

6.   Find something you like about everyone that you know and everyone that you meet.

7.   Schedule time by yourself to think and to write affirmations. This will make it easy to become your own best friend and give up being your own date of last resort.

NOTICE HOW WEALTHY YOU ALREADY ARE

If money is a survival issue for you, it is a good idea to notice that lack of money has not killed you. If you pay taxes in your city, then you own the public transportation systems there. The bus driver is being paid with your money to provide a useful service for you. For fifty cents or so you can ride on the bus anytime you want to and you don't have to worry about taking care of the bus when you are done using it.

When you spend seventy-five cents for a container of milk at the super market, consider that the super market has thousands of dollars worth of refrigerators there so that you get the milk at exactly the right temperature. The plant where the milk was processed probably has millions of dollars worth of equipment as does the dairy farm of origin. You are able to receive the benefits of all this for 75¢.

DEMOLISHING A POVERTY CONSCIOUSNESS

Here is an exercise that will rapidly destroy a poverty consciousness.Make a list of your ten most negative ideas about money. Select the most negative one and invert it into an affirmation that you want to work with. Do not be fooled by the simplicity of this exercise. With my consulting clients I have found that this exercise is the most effective one, which is why I have saved it for last.

Here is a space to do this:

Negative thoughts	Affirmations
1.	1.
2.	2.
3.	3.
4.	4.
5.	5.
6.	6.
7.	7.
8.	8.
9.	9.
10.	10.

CHAPTER VI

Common Causes of Poverty Consciousness

In my consulting work, I have discovered several common causes of poverty consciousness. What follows is a description of each case as well as the affirmations that have enabled people to get free of it. Since everyone is different, this chapter should not be considered to contain all the causes of poverty consciousness. In reading this chapter, I suggest that you study the symptoms and see whether they apply to you. If they do, I suggest you take the applicable affirmations.

FAILING TO GET EVEN

This is the most common cause of poverty consciousness. All parents secretly or openly desire their children to be more successful than they are. As children, frequently the only way to get the attention of our parents is to do what they disapprove of. This is certain to bring attention in the form of correction. We resent this correction because no one likes to feel helpless or be told what to do. For most children, it is not safe enough to express this resentment. You may have tried to tell your parents what you thought about their ideas about bringing you up and found the results unpleasant for you. When you grow up it finally becomes safe enough to express the resentment you felt during childhood. An easy way to do this is to fail financially and have your parents live in continuing fear of having to support you or to feel responsible for your failure as you attempt to demonstrate to them what a poor job they did as parents. Failing to get even (I hope you did not miss the play on words) can take forever. Since there is no satisfaction in it, it will never feel like you got even enough. If you resent authority figures, if you resent rich people or if

41

you are one of those people who loves your parents and considers them perfect, then you probably have some of Failing to Get Even.

Affirmations
1. I forgive my parents for their ignorant behavior toward me.
2. It is OK for me to accept love and money now and still get even later if I want to.

FEAR OF LOSS OF PARENTS' LOVE

If there was not much physical affection expressed in your household as a child and instead your parents expressed their love for you by giving you things like cars, vacations and clothes, then you probably have some of this syndrome. Receiving gifts from your parents is the way you get their love, so you keep yourself poor, or at least poorer than they are so you will always be in a position to receive gifts from them. This syndrome sometimes manifests in what I call the Income Ceiling Law. I have worked with clients who several times during their careers have increased their income up to what the maximum family income of their parents was only to have their income inexplicably decrease. To observe this pattern, it is usually necessary to add a couple of thousand dollars per year to the maximum income of the parents to allow for inflation, because it is really income as reflected in standard of living that matters here.

In other cases, of this syndrome, people are chronic overachievers, but never seem to be satisfied. This is you if you are your own worst critic.

Affirmations
1. I deserve love whether I am successful or not.
2. It is safe for me to be imperfect.
3. It is OK and safe for me to make more money than my parents.

INHERITED MONEY

It is not necessary to come from a family where large inheritances are part of the family tradition or to ever have received an inheritance in order to have this syndrome. If as a small child, you were promised an inheritance of $500 that probably sounded like a huge fortune to you at the time. It is interesting to notice that in families where inheritances are part of the family tradition, frequently everyone knows how much everyone will receive when everyone dies, but when I ask the people about this they claim that they never talk about it. A family tradition of inherited money frequently involves guilt, helplessness and loss associated with money. I have seen people who have been promised small inheritances feel so guilty about just the prospect of profitting from the loss of a loved one that they kept themselves poor for years so they could feel like they would deserve the inheritance when it came. Unravelling this syndrome is a two-step process. The first step is to take responsibility for the money that you have received as an inheritance so that you can let go of the guilt and helplessness surrounding it. The second step is to dissolve the subconscious association between dollars and death. Here are some affirmations so that you can do that:

1. I deserve to be prosperous and wealthy.
2. It is OK for me to receive love and money from various people and places at once.
3. My wealth contributes to my aliveness and to the aliveness of others.

HELPLESSNESS

Helplessness is the thought that you can't get what you want—or that getting what you want is so difficult that it is not worth it. If, as a child, rewards were always contingent upon the performance of some unpleasant task—no allowance until you mow the lawn, no ice cream until you eat your lima beans, then you probably have some of this syndrome. The basic idea is that in order to get what you want, you have to give up your freedom. Obviously, your freedom is more valuable than money, so the tendency here is to stay poor.

Affirmations
1.　My wealth contributes to my freedom and my freedom contributes to my wealth.
2.　I have enough time, energy, wisdom and money to accomplish all my desires.

WOMEN AND MONEY

I have worked with women whose only negative idea about money is that money is something that men do, and women should have nothing to do with it. Women's Lib notwithstanding, if you are a woman, you probably grew up with different ideas about money than your twin brother did or than your twin brother would have if you had had one. Money responds to the commands of your mind and it knows nothing about your gender. There is nothing to stop you from becoming a millionaire and keeping your sexual attractiveness, too. The archetype of the mindless housewife is fast disappearing from the American scene. Even when it existed, the mindless housewife was not so mindless as she was led to believe; it is just that she forgot to acknowledge herself for the managerial skill she exhibited in orchestrating the complex transportation, food service, entertainment and personal counselling business required to run a home.

Affirmations
1. I am no longer a helpless victim. I have the right to tell myself and others what to do.
2. I am not my mother. I am a financially successful business woman.
3. It is fun for me to be a wealthy woman.

MEN AND MONEY

If you are a man, you may feel that you have been blessed with more training about money than your sisters. Unfortunately, if you think about it, you will discover that the majority of this training is negative, and has to do with struggle and control. A common idea held by men is that if they amass a fortune, it will ensure their financial security and they will then be able to relax. Since most tension is psychosomatic, rather than financial, they don't feel any more relaxed after they have the money.

Affirmations
1. I feel safe whether I am in control or not.
2. Past negative experiences no longer detract from my financial success.
3. It is fun for me to be a wealthy man.

DEBT AS A CONDITON OF LIFE

If your parents were in debt until they died and it was only the life insurance money that solved their financial problems, you may have this syndrome. It is your fear of death that is keeping you in debt.

Affirmations

1. My income exceeds my expenses whether I like it or not.
2. I forgive my parents for their financial problems.
3. I am a financial success since my income has exceeded $_____ this year. (Insert the amount of income you have received in the past 12 months in the affirmation.)

UNDERNOURISHMENT SYNDROME

If you were not breast fed as an infant or were fed on a pre-determined schedule, you may have some of this syndrome. You may have concluded "There is not enough milk" or I have to wait for what I want". These ideas are later translated into "There is not enough money."

People with this syndrome often have an abundance of money everywhere but in their pocket or experience widely varying income patterns from month to month. The basic idea here is that nourishment is something beyond your control.

Affirmations

1. I forgive my mother for her unwillingness to nourish me at birth.
2. I am now certain that there is enough for me.

CHAPTER VII

The Spending Law

The SPENDING LAW can also be called the Exchanging Law or the Giving Law. The SPENDING LAW STATED IS—

THE VALUE OF MONEY IS DETERMINED BY THE BUYER AND SELLER IN EVERY TRANSACTION.

Mastery of this law will relieve you from guilt about money from the fear of cheating others and from the fear of being cheated yourself.

Affirmations regarding the SPENDING LAW

1. My income now exceeds my expenses.
2. The more willing I am to prosper others, the more willing others are to prosper me.
3. Every dollar I spend comes back to me multiplied.

Affirmations regarding the SPENDING LAW—explained

"My income now exceeds my expenses." A basic principle about money is that you must receive it before you spend it. This means that you have and have always had a positive cash flow. If you have money in your pocket, in your piggy bank, in your checking account or anywhere else, then that money is the degree to which your cash flow is positive. Even if you have bills to pay, your cash flow is positive. Even after you pay your bills, your cash flow is positive. Banks make it easy for you to see this, because if you pay bills in excess of the cash in your checking account, they will return some checks to you with a note that says in effect "Since you always have a positive cash flow, it is impossible for us to pay these checks yet." Bills and debts are not expenses, they are agreements. Bills and debts do not become expenses until you pay them. You will find practical ideas for handling bills and debts in the next chapter which is about Budgeting. My income now exceeds my expenses happens to be the truth about money whether you like it or not. Working with this affirmation will incorporate it into your consciousness at the emotional level.

"The more willing I am to prosper others, the more willing others are to prosper me." The essence of practicing this idea is the act of generosity. Generosity is the willingness to give money freely to people that do not need it. This is different from the practice of charity which is the willingness to give money freely to people that do need it. Charity is a wonderful idea and a noble practice, but it will not get you out of need for money. Generosity is the fastest way I can think of to get out of need for money. Need equals lack equals shortage. Sometimes people think their need for money is what creates money for them. This idea makes it difficult to give up your need because you are certain if you give up your need for money, it will stop coming to you. If you think you need money, this thought is an affirmation of your lack, your shortage. Regularly giving money to people who don't need it will dissolve any mental association you may have between money and need. If you cannot find someone who does not need money right away, then give it to someone who has provided value for you in your life. You can be sure that they will use the money for something valuable.

"Every dollar I spend comes back to me multiplied." The concept behind this affirmation is profit. Spending money puts it into circulation and the dollar that you spend goes through many transactions before it returns to you. Each transaction produces a profit. Profit is the multiplication factor that operates on your expenses so that more will return to you. Profit can be defined as the creation of new wealth by the arbitrary decree of the individual business person. If you buy something for 50¢ and sell it for a dollar, your profit is 50%, but you could have sold it for 60¢ or for $10, in which case your profit would have been different.

PRICES

The topic of prices deserves explanation because it is a

48

source of confusion about money. If you visit the local hamburger stand and ask why a Super Burger with Cheese costs 89¢, you might get an answer like—'Well, we take the cost of the meat, the cost of the bun, the cost of the tomato and add them up and multiply the sum by 1.2. Then we take the cost of the rent, the cost of the people to cook and serve it, and the cost of the electricity; we add these numbers together and multiply the sum by 1.3. The final step is to take the two final numbers and add them together which produces an answer of 89¢. So that is why Super Burgers with Cheese cost 89¢.'

If you examine this answer a little, you will discover the truth about prices. This is that all prices are arbitrary. Even the prices that are determined by formula are arbitrary because the formulas are arbitrary. Considering the case of the Super Burger with Cheese, the costs that are included and omitted from the formula are abritrary, the factors in the formula are arbitrary and the allocation of common costs to each product is arbitrary.In fact, if you visit another hamburger stand across the street from the first one, you may get an entirely different answer whether their price for a Super Burger with Cheese is the same or different.

NEGOTIATION

Since all prices are arbitrary, then all prices are negotiable. In fact, everything in the physical universe is negotible. Negotiation is the process whereby both parties to a transaction get what they want. In economic terms it is the practice that converts the general marketplace to the specific marketplace. More than one person is required for there to be a transaction. Transactions never occur without the agreement of two or more people. Anyone who has ever been involved in a real estate transaction is aware of this. You can make a detailed study of the real estate market in your neighborhood to arrive at the best asking price for your house. All of that study does not do you a bit of good until you have an offer from a buyer; from someone who agrees with you. The secret of negotiation is to find out what you want and ask for it, then find out what the other person wants and figures out a way to give that in exchange. I find it humorous that it is more socially acceptable in most circles to complain about what you have than it is to ask for what you want.

The fear of being trapped into a deal that they don't like is what prevents most people from negotiating. You have the right to say no at any point in a negotiation, whether you explain the reason for the no or not. Additionally, all agreements are subject to renegotiation at any point. You could not make an agreement unless you had the power to make agreements and making an agreement does nothing to take away that power.

CREDIT

There are several paradoxes about credit. Credit is for people who don't need it, it is for people with enough imagination to put the money that they borrow to effective use. If you don't believe this, try to get a loan without filling out an application that describes how you will repay the money. This is, in essence, an attempt on the part of the banks to teach you the principles in this book.

Conversely, if you borrow enough money from the bank and you have trouble making the payments, they will loan you more to make the payments with. This is because you have gotten to the point where they can't afford to have you go under.

The best policy regarding credit is to pay cash for everything except self-liquidating assets. This means you have to figure out how to create a profit on any item that you borrowed money for so you can repay the loan and have some extra for yourself. Personal charge cards are the bane of people with a poverty consciousness. If charge cards are a problem for you, I recommend that you cut them up in little pieces and immediately begin the practice of paying cash for everything except self-liquidating assets. Master Charge is a wonderful idea, but if you are buying things that you would not otherwise buy because you have the card, then the card is the master of you instead of the other way around. In *Think and Grow Rich* Napoleon Hill wrote "The spendthrift cannot succeed, mainly because he stands eternally in fear of poverty. Form the habit of systematic saving by putting aside a definite percentage of your income. Money in the bank gives one a very safe foundation. . . .

Without money, one must take what one is offered, and be glad of it."

$100 BILL

This little idea is great for people who are always saying 'I don't have any money.' Visit the bank and get a $100 bill and carry it in your pocket or purse. You can spend it whenever you want to so long as you can replace it from the bank immediately. If you follow this practice, you will never be broke again. You will never get down to your last dollar. The closest you will ever get to being broke is your last $100. The reason that people stay broke for so long is that it is depressing to be broke, however it is difficult to be depressed with $100 in your pocket. If $100 is too scary for you, you can start the practice with a silver dollar or a two dollar bill and graduate yourself upwards as you become more confident with money.

TAXES, ECONOMICS, AND THE MONEY SYSTEM

It is a popular practice of financially unsuccessful people to blame the government for their financial problems. A study of economic history will indicate that there have been a wide variety of political philosophies and economic doctrines that have achieved popularity in different countries at different times. Despite all this, there have always been some people with more money than others. It is impossible to make any economic system the cause of financial success or failure.

Money was invented by people for their own convenience. $100 dollar bills are easier to carry around, to exchange and to store than the goods and services that they represent. Articles of value in any economy are the goods and services that the people exchange with each other. Money is the *measure* not the essence of this value.

If the economic system were to disappear then someone would have to re-invent another one. I like to ask people who blame the economic system for their problems what it is that makes them think they will do any better with a different system.

Inflation is an obvious example of the power of the human

mind over money. Inflation occurs because everyone thinks that it will. This expectation makes it a self fulfilling prophecy.

It is interesting to me that those who complain the most about taxes claim not to be interested in politics. If having 30-50% of your income taken out of your pay check before you even see it is not enough to get you interested in politics; what will it take? The validity of your complaints about the government is questionable if you do not vote. The wisdom of your opinions is wasted if you do not communicate them to your elected representatives.

TITHING

Tithing is an ancient prosperity principle. Tithing is regularly giving away ten percent of your income. Giving away ten percent of your income produces several beneficial effects. This practice provides the opportunity to confront any thoughts you may have about lack of money, it helps you feel that you actually own the remaining ninety percent of your income instead of having your income already "spoken for" by other people, and it helps to free you from needing money.

CHAPTER VIII

The Monthly Percentage Budget

The purpose of the Monthly Percentage Budget is to realize that you are cause in money. Dollar budgets do not work because they operate from scarcity. If you ever did a dollar budget, you probably thought 'Since I do not have enough money, I'd better make a budget.' After adding up your expenses, you found out that your worst fears were true, that you really didn't have enough money. A Percentage budget will work for you every time if you practice it faithfully. This is because it starts with the idea of abundance. Another important result that the budget will produce for you is certainty about your ability to live abundantly within your means no matter what your means may be. This is important because without this certainty, money is always an emergency for you and it is more difficult to produce creative ideas when you are in an emergency.

The first step in the creation of a Monthly Percentage Budget is to make a list of the items that you spend money for. Consolidate these categories into logical classifications so that there are approximately 8-10 categories.

Sample Monthly Percentage Budget

Savings	10%
Debts	20%
Gifts	10%
Taxes	15%
Housing	15%
Self-Improvement	10%

Food	12%
Transportation & Communication	8%
	100%

The second step is to assign percentages of your monthly income to spend in each of these categories as shown in the sample. I was so unconscious about my expenses that I found it necessary to keep a record of all the cash that I spent for a month before I felt confident enough to prepare a Monthly Percentage Budget.

The final step is the ongoing practice of finding ways that you can reduce your expenditure in each category while at the same time living better in that category. A good way is to select one category and think about it until you have successfully produced a surplus in that category before moving on to the next one. Once you have figured out how to live better in one category for less money, you have secured a surplus for yourself in that category for future months because you will certainly not want to go back to whatever you were doing before which not only cost more but produced less satisfaction.

Remember, every time you spend money, you increase the income of someone else. Taken to an extreme, if you had a successful business in every area where you now spend money, it would be possible to reduce your expenses to zero.

EXPLANATION OF ITEMS IN THE SAMPLE MONTHLY PERCENTAGE BUDGET

SAVINGS

Once you develop the habit of saving 10% of your income you will never be without money. As shown in the budget it is important to save the *first* 10% of your income. This is merely building the habit of paying yourself first. Do not wait until you can afford to save 10% before beginning this practice. Actually you cannot afford not to begin this practice immediately, if you haven't already done so. This is because saving regularly is an affirmation that you have a surplus of cash which will have a favorable effect on your income. Do not wait until you are out of debt to become a successful saver.

DEBTS

If you have debts, then I suggest that you put aside no more than 20% of your monthly income for debt payments. It is a good idea to make regular payments to each one of your creditors, no matter how small the payments are. If you have a debt that you are not making payments on, it is very easy to figure out how long it will take you to repay it at that rate. The answer is FOREVER. If the monthly payments on your debts exceed 20% of your income, then it becomes necessary to negotiate with your creditors and to work out a payment plan that will enable you to win. Sometimes I have seen people continue to make large regular payments on their debts which they could ill afford solely in order to protect their credit rating. If you have debt problems, the last thing you need to worry about is your credit rating which got you into the mess in the first place. In fact, honest communication with your creditors and regular monthly payments, both of which are indications of your ability and willingness to repay, are the fastest ways to increase your credit rating.

GIFTS

Having gifts as a category in your budget will enable you to practice generosity as described in the previous chapter.

TAXES

If you are self-employed, then it is a good idea to put aside a portion of your income for taxes, so that you have money to pay them when the time comes. It is much easier to negotiate with the IRS for a lower tax bill if you are not starting at the point of being unable to pay what the IRS may think you owe. If your employer withholds income taxes from your salary then this category is taken care of for you.

HOUSING

There are a myriad of ways to reduce your housing expense and to live better. Here is a list of some of the ideas that people have used. You can pick one or more that you like or invent your own according to personal preference. Acquire enough real estate so that the income from it pays your rent, find a housemate that you like, use your house for your business or buy your own home if you now rent, make energy saving investments in your home.

SELF-IMPROVEMENT

Self-improvement is the best investment you can make because you are investing directly in yourself. Conversely, rent is the worst investment you can make, because all you get is shelter for 30 days. At the end of the month your landlord wants some more money. The money you spent on this book, on other self-improvement books and on self-improvement seminars and courses will provide you dividends forever and at no extra charge.

CLOTHING

Here again are some ideas that people have used to have better clothing and to spend less. Make your own, find a job you like better that requires cheaper clothing, select a clothing store and tell them how much you want to spend on clothing every month and say you are willing to spend it all at their store if they will give you a discount. When you find a store that will agree to it, open a charge account and mail them the money in your clothing budget every month. When you want to go shopping, simply look at the credit balance in your charge account to see how much you have to spend.

FOOD

I know of a woman in New York who visited Tiffany's and ordered fancy engraved invitations that invited her to dinner. She mailed them out to all her friends and asked them to fill in a date and time that was convenient for them and to mail them back to her. This is surely an act of high self esteem. Those who think that their company is a nuisance would never think of something like this.

TRANSPORTATION AND COMMUNICATION

Car pool, hitchhike, buy your plane tickets far enough in advance to get a discount, fly at night, carry interesting things to sell on the plane, make your phone calls at night, call collect,use the mail system instead of the phone, etc., etc.

The fact that most of us are pretty unconscious about what we spend our money on makes it easy for a percentage budget to have a dramatic and rapid effect on your expenses. There is no limit to the ideas that will work for you here. If you think that some of your expenses are fixed, then ask yourself who it was that fixed them.

SPENDING AND RESENTMENT (or how to have a successful financial relationship with your lover)

The safety that we feel in intimate relationships frequently allows thoughts and feelings about money to come to the surface that we are not in touch with in other relationships. I am not going to tell you what the best financial arrangements are for your household; but I can tell how to arrive at the financial arrangement that will be most harmonious for you. The way to do this is to experiment. Most people handle money in their relationships the same way that their parents did. Unless your parents' financial life together was totally harmonious, then it might be worthwhile for you to experiment a little. Parental arguments about money frequently give people the idea that money is not a socially acceptable topic of conversation because of the upsets that are caused by discussing it.

Here are a couple of mind-expanding ideas about money in relationships. If the woman is the one who stays home and takes care of the house (A recent Government survey tells me that only 34% of American adult females are in this category) and the man is the only income producer; then it is reasonable for her to receive a salary for the household managerial services she provides. If he objects, then she can suggest that he look in the local newspaper to find out how much live-in maids cost these days. Conversely, if the man is the only income producer and pays the rent or mortgage payments; then there is no reason that the woman should not pay rent. I always recommend that both parties in an intimate relationship have their own checking and savings accounts. Joint checking usually turns into a race— a race to see who can spend the money first or a race to see who can be the most martyrous about not spending it.

Successful negotiation can be accomplished by having a financial discussion with your partner at regularly scheduled intervals (the beginning of the month seems to be a good time). At this discussion you make agreements about who will pay how much of each of the expenses. This is a reasonably risk free way to do it, even if both of you are afraid about negotiating because the agreement only lasts for a month. At the beginning of the next month you will have had a month's experience with the agreement you made and an opportuntiy to make a different one or just change parts of it, if you want to.

Being clear about money with your partner will reduce upset and confusion in your relationship and will add to the joy and freedom of being together.

CHAPTER IX

The Saving Law

THE SAVING LAW can also be called the Storing Law or the Surplus Law. THE SAVING LAW is storing away part of your current income for the purpose of future leisure or to increase your future income. If you have the ability to save regularly it is an indication that you are at least as intelligent as a squirrel who stores away nuts for the winter. The Federal Savings and Loan League tells me that most people are not apparently this intelligent. In a recent survey of thousands of savings accounts, the Federal Savings and Loan League discovered that 90% of the accounts surveyed were dormant after being open for six months. This means they had a balance of $10 or less and that there was no one making deposits or withdrawals. So, if you master saving you will become a member of the elite.

If you want to, you can depress yourself into becoming a successful saver by adding up all the money you have ever earned and comparing that to the balance in your savings account.

I think that the reason that so many people fail at savings is because they have only one savings account. If you only have one savings account then you are saving without purpose or you are saving for the money. I would call this hoarding or saving for a rainy day or saving out of fear of running out. The secret of saving successfully and easily is to have multiple savings accounts each with a special purpose. Here is a list of the seven savings accounts that I recommend. A little later I will describe the secrets of each one.

1. Large Purchases Savings Account

2. Financial Independence Savings Account
3. Millionaire's Savings Account
4. Annual Income Savings Account
5. Cash Flow Savings Account
6. Taxes Savings Account
7. Generosity Savings Account

LARGE PURCHASES SAVINGS ACCOUNT

The purpose of the Large Purchases Savings Account is to keep it empty. Deposit money into it regularly and withdraw the money for any purpose that you wish. Incidentally, this is the account that people with a single savings account usually have, however they have usually not given themselves permission to spend the money whenever they want to, so they end up beating themselves up when they make a withdrawal.

FINANCIAL INDEPENDENCE SAVINGS ACCOUNT

The purpose of the Financial Independence Savings Account is to become financially independent. Financial independence is having enough money coming in every month so that you can live in the style that you are accustomed to whether you work or not. Once you get in this position, your income will increase very rapidly because it is clear that you are working out of choice. The Financial Independence Savings Account has two rules that go with it:

1. Never remove the principal.
2. Spend the interest regularly.

If you remove the principal you will become less instead of more financially independent every month. It is a good idea to ask your bank to mail you the interest from this account. The first interest check I received from my financial independence account was $3.63. At first, I was not very impressed about how financially independent I was, until I realized that a check for at least this much would be coming to me every quarter (four times per year) forever. I took the day off, cashed my check and spent the afternoon at the movies watching a double feature matinee and spent all that time feeling what it felt like to be financially independent.

I call the income from my Financial Independence Savings Account "Eternal Regular Income" because it comes to me no matter what I do and will continue to do so forever.

MILLIONAIRE'S SAVINGS ACCOUNT

The purpose of the Millionaire's Savings Account is to become a Millionaire. The fastest way to become a millionaire is to master the FOUR LAWS OF WEALTH including the INVESTMENT LAW. The Millionaire's Savings Account is to accumulate cash to make investments. The rule it has is that you only withdraw money for the purpose of making investments.

ANNUAL INCOME SAVINGS ACCOUNT

The purpose of the Annual Income Savings Account is to accumulate an annual income so that you can take a year off. Although I recommend that everyone have an Annual Income Savings Account, this account is an especially important one for self-employed people who like their work so much that they never have time for vacations. There are several interesting ways that you can play with this account. One is to accumulate two day's income in it and then take a paid vacation day, paying yourself one day's income. You will have a day off and still have a day's income in the account when you return to work. Then accumulate four day's income and take two paid vacation days and so forth until you have graduated yourself to taking a year off.

Another way is to deposit 10% of your income into this account every pay period. Once per month withdraw 10% of the *balance* of this account and take a vacation for as much time as the money allows. This practice will cause both the balance in this account and your paid vacation time every month to increase.

Still a third way is to deposit 10% of your income into this account every pay period and allow it to accumulate until you have enough to take a year off. Mathematically it will take 6 to 7 years with interest to accumulate an annual income by saving

10% in this account. However you will probably discover that the impact of the growing balance upon your consciousness will at least cut this time in half.

CASH FLOW SAVINGS ACCOUNT

The purpose of the Cash Flow Savings Account is basic training in savings. If you deposit your income into your checking account then you must make another decision in order to save any of it. This is because as everyone knows, checking accounts are for spending, not for saving. If you have followed the practice of depositing your income to your checking account, paying your bills and then intending to save what is left over, you probably already know that there is rarely much left over to save. A Cash Flow Savings Account will solve this problem. You use this account by depositing all of your income into your Cash Flow Savings Account as soon as you receive it. When you want money for your budget or to feed your other savings account, then make a withdrawal and distribute the money to your checking account and other savings accounts. The key is to *always make the withdrawals smaller than the deposits*. When you follow this practice, inexorable mathematical law will cause the balance in this account to increase. Soon the increasing balance in your Cash Flow Savings Account will be a month's income. Having a balance equivalent to a month's income in your Cash Flow Savings Account will make a significant contribution toward your being able to stop worrying about money. I suggest that on the first of the month, you withdraw your month's income from your Cash Flow Savings Account and deposit it into your checking account. At this point, you can be certain of having no financial problems at all for thirty days. During the month you can use the money in your checking account for your budget and can be depositing your income into your cash flow account which will be intact at the beginning of the next month. To some this may sound like financial hocus pocus, which it is until you examine the psychological factors involved. The practice of spending last month's income this month removes you from hope about money. (Hope is an emotional state that is questionably more comfortable than worry.) No longer will you be thinking, 'I hope the heating bill does not arrive until after pay day' or 'I hope this customer pays me soon so I can pay my rent.'

TAXES SAVINGS ACCOUNT

The purpose of the Taxes Savings Account is to accumulate cash so that you can pay your taxes when the time comes. If you are self-employed, it is a good idea to compute your tax liability monthly and to deposit enough cash into this account to cover it.

GENEROSITY SAVINGS ACCOUNT

The purpose of the Generosity Savings Account is to accumulate cash so that you can make large cash gifts to people. If you are already practicing generosity then you know that giving away cash is very different from giving other kinds of gifts. Giving away cash requires that you give up any ideas that you may have about what might be good for the recipient or what it is that they need to have. You will find that generosity will enable you to let go of your desire to control others and will increase your ability to express your love freely, instead of looking for something in return.

GETTING STARTED WITH SAVING

I suggest that all of your savings accounts be passbook accounts. If you travel a lot you may want your Cash Flow Savings Account to be a statement savings account so that you can make frequent deposits by mail without waiting for the passbook to come back to you. According to personal preference, the accounts can all be at the same bank or all at different banks or any combination.

Here is a little trick that helped me to build the habit of regular savings when I was getting started. Pick one of the first four savings accounts listed at the beginning of this chapter. The trick is to have the Post Office remind you when it is time to save. You write out a check to the account that you have selected and mail it with the passbook to the bank. When the passbook comes back to you, mail in another deposit before you go to sleep that night. Another way of expressing this is that the

63

passbook never sleeps at my house. Even if you can afford to deposit only a dollar when it is time to save, it is still worthwhile to do it. The regularity of the practice is the important thing here, not the size of the deposits. In fact, if you only deposit a dollar per week in each of your accounts, you will be doing more toward becoming a successful saver than if you put $200 once a month into one of them. The ultimate truth about saving is that saving has nothing to do with money; this is because regular saving is an affirmation that you have more money than you need and if you have more money than you need now then you will always have more money than you need, so you will never need the money that you are saving.

Affirmations about Saving
1.   A part of all I earn is mine to keep.
2.   Every day my income increases whether I am working, playing or sleeping.

A FINAL WORD OF CAUTION

Do not save for emergencies. If you do this then you are ordering your mind to create emergencies for yourself so you can spend the money that you have saved.

CHAPTER X

The Investing Law

The INVESTING LAW can be thought of as a combination of the first three LAWS OF WEALTH. THE INVESTING LAW is spending your capital in your name with the purpose of earning a higher return than the savings and loan pays you. I want to point out that it is not my purpose to tell you what you should invest in.

In the next four chapters, I will discuss several common investment opportunities, provide you with ways to be successful regardless of what you invest in, and describe how to select the best investment opportunity for you. Contrary to popular opinion, it does not require a large sum of capital to become a successful investor. Many people who have attended my seminars have used the principles that I describe in this book to start their own successful business with an investment of less than $100.

BASIC INVESTING PRINCIPLES

Money follows the commands of your mind exactly. This is true regardless of the financial activity that you engage in. It is true at your job, your business, in the stock market, in the gambling casino and at the racetrack. The basic affirmation about investing is: ALL MY INVESTMENTS ARE PROFITABLE. Your mind has the ability to make any percentage of your investments profitable, so why not 100%?

Eliminate worry from your investing. There are several ways to do this. Use your imagination to:

1. Find investments that you will not worry about.
2. Find creative ways to manage your investments so that

your maximum loss is set at an amount that you will not worry about.

3. Use affirmations to process out your psychoanalytic fear of loss.

4. Invest only in things you love.

Manage your investment cash so that you can stay in the investment business forever. Surely this is long enough for anyone to learn to be a successful investor.

EXPLANATION OF BASIC INVESTING PRINCIPLES

If you have made same unsuccessful investments in the past, it is important to let go of any desire you may have left to blame other people or other forces outside yourself for your losses. As long as you are blaming your losses on the market, the stockbroker, the real estate agent, your parents or a book you read, it is impossible for you to become a successful investor until you change these outside factors that you are blaming. Since you have little or no direct control over these outside factors, it is difficult to be a successful investor as long as you think that your results are affected by anything other than yourself.

Worrying about your investments will not increase your success. Even if you are successful with investments that you worry about, the ulcers and other physical tensions, will not make it worth it. The international economy offers a broad range of investment opportunities and will continue to do so. It is not necessary for you to master them all at once. Examples of investment opportunities:

Your Own Business—This can be anything that you can imagine.

Real Estate—Your own home, income property, real estate investment trusts, limited partnerships, vacation property, undeveloped property.

Securities—Government bonds, municipal bonds, corporate bonds, preferred stock, common stock, common stock options, commodities futures, currency speculation, commodities options, personal loans, second mortgages.

Personal Property—Art collections, rare coins, books and

stamps, precious metals and gems, antique cars.

Certainly there are investment opportunities available everyday that are not listed here. Each one of the investment opportunities that I have listed has a different risk profile and a different degree of liquidity.

Money is the commodity that investing is conducted with. For this reason, it is important to learn to manage your investment capital in a way that you can stay in the investment business forever. This first principle is:

Always keep a portion of your investment capital in reserve.

This means you should never invest the entire balance of your Millionaire's Savings Account, so that you will always have cash to make investments. The second principle can be stated in affirmation form:

I always divide my profits into current expenses, financial independence, investments and reserves.

Let's say you invest $6000 in the stock market and realize a $2000 profit. When the sale is completed, you have $8000; the $6000 you started with and $2000 in profit. You have already paid taxes on the $6000, but in most cases the $2000 is at least partially taxable. You can be certain of always having cash to invest if you return the $6000 of original capital to your Millionaire's Savings Account and divide the remaining $2000 (the profit) into four categories. The amount you put into each category is up to you.

1.   Current expenses including taxes. Spend a portion of every profit you make so that your profits are not eternally re-invested and to reward yourself for being a good investor.

2.   Financial Independence Savings Account. Deposit a portion into your Financial Independence Savings Account so that every profitable investment contributes to your Eternal Regular Income.

3.   Take a portion of your profit and invest it in something else. This is the principle of diversification or spreading of investment risk to multiple investments. If you don't have an immediately available investment opportunity, you can place this portion of your profit into your Millionaire's Savings

Account, until you find another investment opportunity.

4. Reserves. Deposit a portion of your profit into your Millionaire's Savings Account so that the capital you have to invest increases with every profitable investment.

OTHER FACTORS IN LEARNING TO INVEST

The fact that you have a sum of investment capital does not obligate you to make investments. I had a client once who hired me to teach her to invest the $500,000 she had just inherited. As she had no experience in investing, I suggested that she have two Millionaire's Savings Accounts and that she put $2000 in one of them and invest that until she had produced a success pattern. In the meantime, the remainder of the money remained intact in her second Millionaire's Savings Account.

It is also important to consider the kind of relationship that you enjoy having before you decide what to invest in. There is no reason that becoming a successful investor should require you to spend time with people whose company you don't like. You will have different relationships with different people if you decide to buy and manage an apartment building than if you decide to be an individual investor in the securities market.

CHAPTER XI

Your Own Business

Having your own successful business is the easiest way to build a success consciousness regarding money. You will find that the success consciousness that you build in your own business can easily be translated into success in real estate, the stock market or any other kind of investing that you want to do. I think that the best investment that you can make is to start a business that is so much fun that you don't care if you go broke. With this approach, you can be certain of success.

SELLING—THE ULTIMATE COMMUNICATIONS WORKSHOP

Fear of selling is what prevents most people from starting their own business and inadequate selling is what causes unsuccessful businesses to fail. I think that a successful sales consciousness should be a requirement for graduating grammar school. This is a revolutionary idea that would put an end to welfare and unemployment permanently. Since most of us did not learn much if anything about selling in our childhood, I am going to suggest a simple training program that makes it easy for anyone to become a successful sales person.

Take a look at your possessions—in your house, car or office— and find a possession that you delight in owning and that has a retail value of $1 to $5. Find out how to get a small supply at the wholesale price. A couple of ways to locate a source of supply are the telephone Yellow Pages, the manufacturer or the retailer where you bought it. For the sake of simplicity we'll say that you select an item that will sell for a dollar and that the wholesale price is fifty cents. Carry several

69

with you in your pocket or purse and give people the opportunity to buy one. This is an easy way to learn how to sell. I have not suggested that you spend your day ringing doorbells selling door to door. It is possible to learn to sell that way, but I think that is the hard way.

It is not necessary to pressure people to sell things. "This is my favorite kind of ball point pen. Not only do they write clearly, but they last for a long time. I am selling them for a dollar. Would you like to buy one?" This type of sales approach makes it fun and easy to sell things.

Selling is giving people the opportunity to buy. All of your fears about selling are wrapped up in what I call the Most Embarrassing Moment. The Most Embarrassing Moment begins when you say "Would you like to buy one?" and it ends when anyone says anything. If you are not going through the Most Embarrassing Moment then you are not selling. Salespeople have come to my house and spent an hour or more in my living room talking about and demonstrating their product without offering me the opportunity to buy. It is a good idea to give the person the opportunity to buy frequently. Do it at the beginning, do it in the middle and do it at the end. Unsuccessful salespeople talk too much and ask too few questions. In the process of learning how to sell successfully you will learn to become a better listener. It is important to ask questions and allow the customer a chance to express himself. Good questions are:

Is that your only objection?
What one do you like the best?
When would you like me to call you again?
Would you like to buy one?

It may be difficult for you to imagine becoming a millionaire selling one dollar items. The point here is to select an item that is so small in price that it does not confront your willingness to receive, so that you can concentrate on learning to sell. You can consider that you have mastered your one dollar item when you sell one every day whether you think about it or not. After you have mastered your one dollar item, you will find that people are approaching you to buy. There is nothing to stop you from becoming a millionaire selling one dollar items. McDonald's is quite successful and they sell very few items that cost more than a dollar.

When you have mastered selling your dollar item you can graduate to a higher priced product if you want to. The consciousness factors and communication skills required to sell dollar items are the same ones that will make you successful in selling $10,000 and $100,000 items. This is indicated by the fact that many of my consulting clients who are real estate agents have doubled their income from real estate commissions by mastering the one dollar item. The process of mastering the one dollar item trained their minds to expect easy and frequent transactions which was translated into their real estate business.

You will find that once you master selling, you will never be short of money again. It is possible to travel wherever you want to and be paid for it. If you think you are good at communicating, then try selling something. Not only will you find out where you have problems in communicating, but the day to day practice will produce rapid improvement in your ability to communicate.

Affirmations about Selling
1. I am an attractive, loving person with money.
2. I am attracting loving people with money to me and they are attracting me.
3. I receive assistance and co-operation from those people everywhere necessary to achieve my desired result.
4. My customers like me.
5. I like my customers.
6. My customers buy from me whether they like me or not.
7. I sell products and services that benefit everyone.
8. I am clever enough to get rejected.
9. If people say no, I never take it personally.
10. The more I sell, the easier it becomes and the easier it becomes, the more I sell.

WINNING IN YOUR OWN BUSINESS

It is a good idea to open a business checking account to

handle your buy and sell business. Use the money in this account to buy inventory and deposit the proceeds of your sales into it. This way it doesn't matter how sloppy your accounting system is, you will be able to see your success. Also it is important to pay yourself a salary, by dividing your profits into the four categories explained in the previous chapter. Several years ago I began buying and selling self-improvement audio cassette tapes. At first I bought my inventory with money in my personal checking account and deposited the money from the sales into the same place. I sold several dozen tapes before I realized that I couldn't find the profit I was making. I knew I must be making a profit, but I couldn't find it because it was disguised by the other transactions in my personal checking account. When I opened a business checking account, just for the tapes, the profit became obvious because the balance in that account kept increasing and I always had a supply of tapes to sell. At that point I had more ideas about how to expand the business than I had money to expand it so I went for several months without paying myself a salary. I found that my sales declined. I decided to pay myself a salary of $10 per month whether the business could afford it or not and the sales began increasing again. If you run your business from the point of view that you are the servant and your business is the master, you are just making it difficult for yourself. You created the business to serve you, and it will serve you if you take the point of view of master.

BUSINESS POLICIES YOU CAN WIN WITH

Getting started. When you start in a service business an easy way to create an abundance of clients is to give away your service at the beginning until you have more clients than you can handle or until people force you to accept money. If you don't like your business well enough to give away your services, this may be an indication to you that you are in the wrong business. When you have an abundance of clients, it is a good idea to continue to give away a portion of your services, even if you have to refuse the money.

Make a Schedule. Create a personal schedule for yourself of

when you want to work with time slots for each client. This way you will be certain of working when you want to. Whenever you have an empty time slot, spend the time figuring out what you could do to fill it.

MONEY BACK GUARANTEE

In any business, it is always wise to offer a money back guarantee. This guarantee is for your benefit, not for the benefit of your clients. When you have a money back guarantee, you will never have to accept money from people unless they are willing to give it to you. This policy will increase your certainty of the willingness of others to prosper you.

ALL PRICES ARE NEGOTIABLE

A willingness to negotiate prices and to accept payment in products and services from your clients will not only expand your business, but will give you increased opportunities to practice your negotiating skills.

Your own business can be thought of as a Money Machine. People with well developed prosperity consciousness find it easy to create a new money machine every day if they want to. With a prosperity consciousness, it does not matter whether your money machine is well oiled or not; you can turn the crank whenever you want to and money will pour out. A prosperity consciousness is the key, however, as many of the businesses that file bankruptcy are well-oiled machines run according to the most scientific, modern business practices except there was no prosperity consciousness.

CHAPTER XII

Investing in Real Estate

If you can afford rent you can afford to own your own home. Rent is the worst investment that you can make. Rent buys you shelter for thirty days, at which point you have to pay it again, with nothing but a cancelled check to show for it.

There are at least three characteristics about real estate that make it easy for you to own your own home. There are: the nature of the expenses of owning real estate, the ease of financing because of the willingness of financial institutions to make loans backed by real estate, and the flexibility of real estate.

THE NATURE OF REAL ESTATE EXPENSES

The primary expenses of owning real estate are principal, interest and taxes. Principal is the money that you repay to the mortgage holder. Since these payments reduce your indebtedness, they are akin to savings. Interest and real estate taxes are deductible on your federal and state income tax. Therefore, depending on your tax rate, the monthly payments that you make for principle, interest and taxes can be 20-100% higher than your present rent and you will be spending the same amount of money for shelter. This is because of the money you save on taxes.

EASE OF FINANCING

Whether you have cash for the down payment or not, it is easy to finance the purchase of a piece of real estate that you want to own. In my consulting with real estate buyers, I have devised several ways to buy real estate without cash. The basic principle is—if you don't have cash or you don't have credit, then use someone else's. With this general principle in mind, you can devise other ways to buy real estate without cash, or use one of these if you want to.

SECOND MORTGAGE

A second mortgage will enable you to borrow the down payment from the seller or another person or from an institution. I have found that asking the seller to take a second mortgage works especially well when the seller has owned the property for a long time. This is because the seller in this case usually has a relatively small balance remaining to pay on his or her mortgage, which reduces the cash required for the seller to complete the transaction. Let's say the purchase price is $40,000 and the seller has a balance of $6,000 remaining on their mortgage and that you are able to obtain 80% financing from the bank. In this case, the buyer would ask the seller to finance the remaining 20% of the purchase price or $8,000. The seller receives the $32,000 in cash that you borrowed from the bank, uses $6,000 of it to pay the balance on the existing mortgage and has $26,000 to put down on his or her next house, plus a regular monthly income from you as you make the payments on the second mortgage.

LEASE WITH AN OPTION TO BUY

A lease with an option to buy will let you have a portion of your rent go towards the down payment of the house you are renting. After you have lived there long enough to have paid enough rent to accumulate a down payment, you can then go to the bank for a mortgage loan to finance the rest. The benefits of this agreement to the seller are having a tenant that likes the house well enough to want to buy it. This will eliminate any problems of vacancies and ensure that the owner has a tenant who will love and care for the property.

SALE/LEASEBACK

Sale/leaseback is a good arrangement when the seller is either unwilling or unable to accept one of the first two approaches. In sale/leaseback you find a third party who is willing to buy the house with conventional terms from the seller and then lease the house to you with an option to buy. For the third party investor, you have the best of all real estate opportunities because he or she can determine the profit that will be made from the entire transaction up to completion when you buy the house, before any money is invested. Additionally the third party investor is assured of having a tenant that will take care of the property and who has a very low likelihood of moving out.

LAND CONTRACT

A land contract works especially well when a regular monthly income is more important to the seller than a lump sum of cash. For example, the seller may own two homes, one of which is being sold. Under a land contract the seller finances the entire amount of the purchase price, which the buyer repays in monthly payments. Let's say that the seller has a house which he or she bought several years ago for $40,000 by making a $10,000 down payment and by giving the bank a mortgage for the remaining $30,000. The house is now for sale for $60,000. As the buyer you give the seller a mortgage for $60,000 and you move in. The seller must continue to make the monthly payments on the $30,000, but assuming approximately equal interest rates and length of mortgage, the payments you make each month to the seller on the $60,000 mortgage will be approximately twice the payment the seller has on the $30,000 mortgage.

INCOME TAX IMPLICATIONS OF BUYING REAL ESTATE WITHOUT CASH

If you research the income tax implications to the seller of any of the transactions I have described, you will discover that the seller usually receives a tax saving compared to selling the real estate by conventional means, and that ultimately the government finances the down payment for the buyer. Every federal administration since Truman has been encouraging Americans to own their own home. It's time to take them up on it.

NEGOTIATING THE TRANSACTION

Frequently in real estate transactions, price is the only variable that is discussed. There are only three things that matter in real estate transactions: 1) terms, 2) terms, and 3) terms. Consider for a moment that with the right terms you could buy the World Trade Center in New York City (assuming you want it). In buying real estate without cash it will be necessary for you to negotiate directly with the seller. The real estate agent can be of assistance to you in your negotiations so it is a good idea to ask him or her to be present at the meetings you have with the seller. As in all negotiations, the way to make the best transaction for all concerned, is to find out what the other person really wants and then figure out the best way for you to give it to them.

THE VALUE OF REAL ESTATE

Real Estate is the simplest investment you can make. After all, it is just a bunch of dirt, sticks and rocks. In the 1870's when gold was plentiful at the height of the gold rush in California, the price of gold was $16 per ounce. Now over 100 years later it sells for about $470 per ounce. This is an average annual increase of about 3% per year. In my experience, it is almost impossible to do worse than that in real estate. The Basic Law of Real Estate Value is that the value of real estate is determined by the income that it produces, be that income psychic or financial. The income that a piece of real estate produces is largely the result of what the real estate is used for. So, the way to increase the value of your real estate is to increase the quality of the ideas that you have about what it can be used for.

An interesting application of this idea can be observed in the introduction of breakfast foods at McDonald's Restaurants. Before the introduction of breakfasts, someone at McDonald's was smart enough to see that there were pieces of real estate all over the country that were being used to serve hamburgers, but that there are only a few people around who have trained themselves to enjoy hamburgers at 7 a.m. The introduction of breakfast foods was a way to increase the cash flow of the company without any additional investment in real estate.

CHAPTER XIII

Investing in Securities

Although this chapter is primarily devoted to investing in common stock, there is nothing to stop you from applying the principles in this book to any kind of securities trading that you want to.

I first became aware of the stock market at age nineteen. At first I was overwhelmed by the amount of knowledge it seemed to require. In fact, the reason that many people are unsuccessful in the stock market is because they immerse themselves in such an uncomprehensible mass of unrelated data that it is almost impossible to sort out the relevant from the irrelevant. The first approach I came up with was to devote my attention and my investing to twenty stocks that I watched closely. Some of them I never invested in, but my attention was focused and I agreed with myself to ignore all information about other stocks no matter how insistent the person was who was trying to give me the information. I was pretty successful with my twenty stock mini-market for two reasons—first my attention was focused and most importantly I was careful to accept responsibility for my results. Since I had selected which stocks I wanted to follow and since I was acting as my own investment advisor, there was no one I could blame except myself when I had a trade that resulted in a loss. Whenever I had a trade that produced a loss I would sit down and examine myself until I found the thought or thoughts that caused it. I knew that if at that point I was only a good enough investor to buy losers, I had better do something to become a better investor before I bought my next stock, or there was no reason that the next one would be anything other than another loser. This is a very interesting way to learn about yourself. If nothing else, you will find out what it means to be certain about your investments.

THE LITTLE OLD LADY APPROACH

Little Old Ladies are very successful in the stock market. Frequent surveys of the ownership of the stock traded on the New York Stock Exchange indicated that over 50% of the shares are owned by females and that the average age of these people is high. So it seems that they must be doing something right. It is paradoxical that the reason that they are so successful is that they do not invest for capital appreciation, instead they invest primarily for income. With my twenty stock mini-market, I had picked the stocks I wanted to watch pretty much arbitrarily and without a system. The Little Old Lady Approach uses three things as qualifying factors for stock selection—these are yield, fundamentals and potential. Before further description, it is necessary to explain these three principles. All the information that you need for this can be found on the Standard and Poor's sheet for the stock in question. These sheets are available at most brokerage offices and public libraries.

YIELD

Yield is the ratio between the annual cash dividend per share paid by a stock and the current market price. The annual cash dividend per share is the money paid by the company directly to the shareholders. The annual dividend is usually paid in four equal payments at three month intervals. The current market price is the price of the stock as of the last trade on the exchange. So, if a company pays an annual cash dividend of $3.20 per share and if the current market price is $40 per share, then the yield is $3.20 divided by $40 or 8%. An important characteristic of the yield is that it varies inversely with the price, so as the price of the stock increases, the yield decreases and vice versa. For example if the price of the stock I just described dropped to $32 per share, the yield would become $3.20 divided by $32 or 10%.

FUNDAMENTALS

Fundamentals are the inherent strength of the company. Especially at the beginning, it is best to invest in companies that have sales in the hundreds of millions of dollars, that show a pattern of increasing sales every year for the last five years and that show a pattern of increasing profits and increasing dividends.

POTENTIAL

Potential will give you an indication of how high you might expect the price of the stock to go. Potential has two dimensions —there is time potential and price potential. To determine the price potential, look at the highest price that the stock has ever sold at. The price potential is the difference between the current price and the highest price expressed as a percentage of the current price. For example, if you have a stock with a current price of $20 per share and an all time high $45 per share, then the difference between the current price and the all time high is $25 and the potential is $25 divided by $20 or 125%. The time potential is how long ago the stock sold at its all time high.

STOCK SELECTION

Start with stocks on the New York Stock Exchange with yields in excess of 7% and examine their fundamentals and potential. You will probably find that a lot of the companies with high yielding stocks are utilities. The major difference between utilities and other companies is that the profits of utilities are regulated by a Government agency. You will be most certain of stocks with strong fundamentals, high price potentials and short time potentials. If the all time high occurred more than five years ago, it is wise to compute another price potential and time potential based on a more recent peak in price.

WHY THE LITTLE OLD LADY
APPROACH WORKS

This works for two reasons; one is that Little Old Ladies are interested in income, not in capital appreciation and the other is that companies that pay dividends consider it important to maintain a stable dividend pattern. For this reason, they are careful to increase the dividend only when they are pretty sure that they can maintain it over the years. After all, if they cut the dividend, they incur the disappointment of those little old ladies who are the shareholders and who would sell their stock if that happened. Although dividend cuts are not unknown, companies with sales in the hundreds of millions of dollars typically have sufficient resources to borrow money to pay dividends, in the event of a temporary slackening in business.

This means that when the price of stocks is high then simultaneously their yields are low. Little Old Ladies look at their portfolios and see that it is yielding 4%. 'I can do better than this at the savings and loan,' they say, so they sell their stock and put the money in the bank while at the same time enjoying an increase in income. More desire to sell than to buy will cause the prices of stocks to go down everytime. As the prices drop, the yields increase. Any Little Old Lady worth her salt would not leave her money in the bank at 5% when there are good stocks to be had that are yielding 8%. So, the money flows out of the savings and loans and back into the stock market, driving the prices back up again. As you can see Little Old Ladies represent the world's largest unorganized mutual fund.

Do not be surprised if hot shot brokers tell you that this approach is too slow, that it will take forever to get rich this way. I don't know any hot shot brokers that support themselves year after year solely on their investment income. Little Old Ladies do it all the time.

MARKET STRATEGY TO AVOID ULCERS

We will assume that you purchased 100 shares of a stock at a price of $40 per share and with a dividend of $3.20 per share. This means that the yield is 8%. The yield acts as a protection against drops in price. If the price drops to $35 per share, then the yield increases to 9%. If your stock was a good buy when it yielded 8% then it is now a better buy and more people will want to buy it. At this point, you should consider buying more; either using the part of the reserve you left in your Millionaire's

Savings Account or if you want to be daring you can buy more by borrowing on the margin from your broker.

As the price increases, I suggest you use stop sell orders so you don't have to worry about your portfolio. A stop sell order is an order to your broker to sell your stock at a specified price. When the price gets to $50 per share, you might want to put in a stop sell order at $46-1/2 per share. This means that you have locked in your profit, because if the price ever drops to $46-1/2 per share, your broker will automatically sell it for you. As the price continues to increase, it is a good idea to keep moving the stop sell order up below the price. Remember to cancel the old stop sell order with your broker. Be careful to put the stop sell order far enough below the current price, so that you will not get sold out by the normal day to day fluctuations of the price of the stock. It is a good idea to plot the prices (High, Low and Close for the day) of the stock for a while to get a feeling of this. If you want to be super conservative, you can start using the stop sell order as soon as you purchase the stock. This simply provides a protection against loss in addition to the yield.

POSTSCRIPT

I want to end with a brief word of encouragement. Courage is not fearlessness. Courage is the willingness to move forward with your fear. Discouragement is when your fear overcomes your intention to move forward. There is no law requiring that you be without fear before acting.

A diligent reading of MONEY IS MY FRIEND is apt to bring to awareness suppressed psychological material from your past. It is a good idea to remember that the past is not only over, but that you survived it. Celebrate the moment. Try writing or recording on cassette the affirmations in this book. I invite you to get your money's worth.

THE VALUE OF READING AND LISTENING

The following books and tapes contain some of the most valuable ideas to be found anywhere. I encourage you to use these products to further your growth and success. Reading and listening is a wonderful and effective way to use the suggestion principle. Take charge of your life; deliberately build a prosperity consciousness now by reading and listening to these and other positive products. Surround yourself with good ideas.

I suggest that you pick one or more of these books and tapes that appeal to you and use it to expand your succcess. Get into the habit of self-improvement. A prosperity and success consciousness is one of the most valuable things you can give yourself.

Copies of this book and additional information about Prosperity Consciousness are available at these locations.

CANADA

VANCOUVER
Gayle Lang
6726 Arbutus St.
Vancouver, B.C. V6P 5S7
604-263-0564

MONTREAL
Micheline Charron
LeLibre-Air
5926 Ave. McLynn
Montreal H3X 2R2
514-340-9019

UNITED STATES

NEW YORK
Bob Mandel
145 W. 87th St.
NY, NY 10024
212-799-7324

PHILADELPHIA
Bill Thompson
2431 Brown St.
Philadelphia, PA 19130
215-765-7958

DALLAS
Ernie Hill
3556 Ridgeoak Way
Dallas, TX 75234
214-247-3430

TEXAS
Michael Hersey
5008 Fresco
Austin, TX 78731
512-459-0255

SEATTLE
MONEY UNLIMITED
10655 NE 4th, #400,
Bellevue, WA 98004
206-453-0302

MINNEAPOLIS
Nick Deach
4601 Excelsior Blvd.
#301
Minneapolis, MN 55416
612-920-3444

SAN FRANCISCO
Yvonne Moriarty
52 El Camino
San Rafael, CA 94901
415-459-1676

MILWAUKEE
Patricia Durovy
2437 N. Booth St.
Milwaukee, WI 53212
414-374-5433

SAN FRANCISCO
Jim Leonard
2224 Seventeenth Ave.
San Francisco, CA 94116
415-753-0370

LOS ANGELES
Trinity Publications
1636 N. Curson Ave.
Hollywood, CA 90046
213-876-6226

AUSTRALIA
Michael West
18/52 Bellevue Rd.
Bellevue Hill 2023
Sydney, NSW
367-5929

ENGLAND
Ben Bartle
143 Willifield Way
London NW11 6XY
01-455-4063

The Door of Everything by Ruby Nelson. $3.95. Published by DeVorss, Marina del Rey, CA. A wonderful statement of Immortalist Philosophy.

How to Live a Greater Life by Paul Gessler. $6.00. San Francisco, CA, self-published. Immortalist workbook leading to the destruction of your personal allegiance to death.

Creative Visualization by Shakti Gawain. $5.95. Published by Whatever Publishing, Mill Valley, CA. A simple and complete description of visualization.

Moneylove by Jerry Gillies. $2.95. Published by Warner Books, New York, N.Y. Particularly good for freeing up your attitudes about money.

The Richest Man in Babylon by George Clason. $2.95. Published by Bantam Books, New York, N.Y. A wonderful primer on the 4 laws of wealth. Written in parables. "A lean purse is easier to cure than to endure."

The Life & Teaching of the Masters of the Far East 5 volumes by Baird Spalding. $4.00 per volume. Published by DeVorss & Co., Marina Del Rey, CA. An account of American scientists who visited and lived with immortal masters in the Himalayas around the turn of the century. Full of uplifting ideas.

Psychological Immortality by Jerry Gillies. $12.95. Published by Richard Marek, New York, N.Y. A synthesis of science and immortalist philosophy. Exercises to expand aliveness.

Physical Immortality by Leonard Orr. $9.95. Published by Celestial Arts, Millbrae, CA. In-depth discussion of immortalist philosophy. An account of the immortal master Herakahn Baba in India. Sociological implications of physical immortality.

SUGGESTED LISTENING

Phil Laut on Cassette!

Money is An Intentional Creation of the Mind. 2 tape set $20.00. Two hour seminar recorded live at the Unity Church in Minneapolis which covers the application of the spiritual principles of forgiveness, service, gratitude, certainty, and integrity to financial life.

Principles of Personal Financial Success. 2 tape set $20.00. Effective use of your mind, your time and your money. Topics include acceptance, affirmations, purpose, motivation, goals, time management, budgeting, saving and investing.

Reclaiming Your Personal Power (Unravelling Infancy Patterns) $10.00. One hour seminar with Phil Laut describing techniques to heal patterns of struggle, dependency and helplessness.

OTHERS

Money Seminar by Leonard Orr. 4 tape set $30.00. Produced by Life Unlimited (see address below). Over 4 hours of positive thoughts about money and prosperity. Recorded live. Covers the 4 laws of wealth, and more.

Live Long and Prosper by Jerry Gillies. $60.00. Produced by Jerry Gillies, Malibu Beach, CA. a 12-part course in abundance and success on 6 cassettes including: Purpose; The Success Habit; The Creative Self; Decision/Commitment; *Take* Your Time; Visualizing Success; and more.

Unravelling the Birth/Death Cycle by Leonard Orr. 2 tape set $18.00. Produced by Life Unlimited, Sacramento, CA. An excellent tape on 2 of the 5 Biggies: Birth and Death.

Prosperity Plus by Rev. Ike. $12.00. Full of positive ideas about money. Contains an excellent success and prosperity visualization.

I Meet No-one But Me by Rev. Ike. 2 tape set $24.00. The truth about life—You create the experiences you have.

The prices listed above are accurate at the time of this printing, and may change. Many of the books are available in bookstores. To make it easy for you, I have arranged with LIFE UNLIMITED to carry all of the products listed above. They have *Money Is My Friend,* and many more excellent titles as well. Write or call for a free catalog.

LIFE UNLIMITED
8125 Sunset #204
Fair Oaks, CA 95628
916-967-2386

TO ORDER THE PRODUCTS LISTED ABOVE:
1. List the titles you want,
2. Include your name and shipping address,
3. Add $1.75 + .35 per title for shipping & Handling.
4. California residents add sales tax.
5. Make your check or money order to
   LIFE UNLIMITED.
OR CALL AND CHARGE IT (Visa or Mastercard). There is a 4% handling fee on Charge card orders.

PROSPERITY CRUISE
with Phil Laut

CRUISE THE CARIBBEAN ON A LUXURY LINER

Have you ever wanted a vacation that continued to give you benefits long after the suntan faded and you were back to the same old grind?

Have you ever wanted a vacation that offered you the opportunity to return with a new sense of purpose and new abilities for accomplishment and satisfaction without struggle?

Phil Laut has been conducting prosperity seminars since 1976. His message of prosperity through the effective use of your mind, your time and your money has reached thousands of people in all parts of the world.

He has the ability to present effective prosperity principles in a humorous and easily understood manner. You will find that his seminars are filled with wisdom, ideas and processes that will serve you for a long time.

Some of the topics covered in the 28 hours of shipboard seminars on this week-long cruise are:

Purpose and Goals
Planning for Success
Your Perfect Career
Accomplishment and Satisfaction without Struggle
Prosperity Thinking
Selling
Budgeting, Savings, Taxes and Investing

1983
Dates   September 18-25
                     Future dates also planned

Total $1380 to $1475
Cost   depending on berthing
             includes $365 cost of seminars *and* round trip fare
             to Miami from U.S. locations.

To Book: Skywing Associates
                     17 Harbor Drive
             Corte Madera, CA 94925 USA
                     415-924-7319

Phil Laut is available to conduct evening and day long seminars as well as weekend trainings. If you would like Phil to appear at your group, church or organization, phone:

213-876-6226

during normal business hours Pacific Time or write: Trinity Publications at 1636 N. Curson Ave., Hollywood, CA 90046

Seminars and Trainings Available
  Life Extension and Physical Immortality Seminar
  Rebirth Seminar
  Self-Analysis Seminar
  Basic Money Seminar
  Rebirthing Training

Money Workshops sponsored by Phil Laut meet weekly in the following locations:

  Dallas TX, contact Billie Ledford, 214-234-5979
  Mexico City, contact Kurt Denker, 905-588-2687 or
    568-5714
  Minneapolis/St. Paul, contact Daniel Berlin, 612-292-0097
  San Francisco, contact Jim Leonard, 415-753-0370
  Vancouver, B.C., contact Gayle Lang and Howard Kiewe,
    604-263-0564

SUGGESTED READING

Rebirthing—The Science of Enjoying All of Your Life by Phil Laut and Jim Leonard. Published by Trinity Publications. Complete, most advanced self-improvement book available anywhere. $7.95.

Think and Grow Rich by Napoleon Hill. $3.00. Published by Wilshire Book Company, North Hollywood, CA. This is a basic primer on money and worthy of repeated reading. Because it was written in 1937, there is little in it about financial freedom for women.

Secret of Unlimited Prosperity by Catherine Ponder. $2.95 Published by DeVorss & Co., Marina Del Rey, CA. An excellent book about tithing.

From Here to Greater Happiness by Joel and Champion Teutsch. $2.95. Published by Price/Stern/Sloan, Los Angeles, CA. A clear and simple explanation of how the mind works. Examples of personal laws in action.

The Creative Process in the Individual by Thomas Troward. $5.95. Published by Dodd, Mead & Co., N.Y., N.Y. This is the best book on metaphysics that I have found. Other books by the same author are good, too. (Dore' Lectures; Edinburgh Lectures; Bible Mystery & Bible Meaning.)

Your Inner Child of the Past by Hugh Missildine. $2.95. Published by Simon and Schuster, N.Y., N.Y. This is the clearest, most loving psychological book about childhood that I have read.

Atlas Shrugged by Ayn Rand. $3.95. Published by New American Library, New York, N.Y. An excellent money book for women.

The Money Game by Adam Smith. $3.95. Published by Random House, New York, N.Y. The best book about the stock market.